SHETLAND
FISHERMEN

SHETLAND FISHERMEN

*Celebrating
50 years of the
Shetland Fishermen's
Association*

James R. Nicolson

Published by
The Shetland Times Ltd.
1999

Shetland Fishermen

Copyright © James R. Nicolson, 1999

ISBN 1 898852 56.1

First published in 1999

This book was commissioned by the Shetland Fishermen's Association
and is published on their behalf by The Shetland Times Ltd.
Shetland Fishermen's Association wishes to acknowledge financial
assistance towards this project from Shetland Enterprise.

Cover design by The Stafford Partnership, Shetland.

British Library Cataloguing-in-Publication Data
A catalogue record for this book is available from the British Library.

Printed and published by
The Shetland Times Ltd.,
Prince Alfred Street,
Lerwick, Shetland ZE1 0EP, UK.

CONTENTS

FOREWORD

It gives me great pleasure to write the foreword to *Shetland Fishermen*. The Shetland Fishermen's Association recently celebrated its fiftieth anniversary and it was decided to commission this book to mark the event. Fishing has dominated the social and economic history of Shetland for hundreds of years. For most of that time Shetland fishermen have been poorly organised and often exploited.

Things started to change early this century when fishermen began to own their own boats. At the same time fishermen saw the need to create a body to represent their interests. Eventually, the Shetland Fishermen's Association was founded in 1947 and has now successfully represented the fishermen of Shetland for over half a century.

I have been a fishermen for most of my working life and count myself fortunate to have been involved with the association for most of my time at sea. I have been chairman of the association since 1996 and feel honoured to follow the many distinguished and hardworking Shetland fishermen who have held this post before me.

As well as marking fifty years of the association, this book charts the fortunes of fishing in Shetland during a period of enormous change. I am particularly pleased that the book concentrates on the people who have worked in the fishing industry during the last half century. The history of fishing in Shetland is rightly the history of the fishermen of Shetland.

The association has had many achievements during its history. To me, its greatest achievement is that it continues to represent virtually every fisherman in the islands, regardless of type or size of boat. It has always been and remains an association for all the fishermen of Shetland. Long may it continue.

Josie Simpson
October, 1999

PREFACE

While the fiftieth anniversary of Shetland Fishermen's Association – in 1997 – provided the inspiration for this book, I decided to take the story a few years farther back, to include the start of seine netting in Shetland as this technique revolutionised the entire white fish industry.

To include every vessel based in Shetland during this period was not the intention. Those mentioned – over three hundred of them – are used to illustrate changes in the industry, either in the size of vessel or in its equipment.

A large number of skippers are named in the book, however it is not a complete "roll of service"; nor is the list of fatalities a complete one.

Local newspapers were the main source of information and I am grateful to archivist Brian Smith for access to the files of *The Shetland News* and to *The Shetland Times* for access to their files.

I wish to thank the many people who have provided information for this book, especially John Goodlad and former skippers Jim Henry, Peter Johnson and Davie Smith, who read the first version of each chapter, noting errors and adding much vital information as the work progressed.

Special thanks are due to Robert Johnson, Martin Smith and others, who submitted the photographs which add so much interest to the book.

James R. Nicolson

CHAPTER ONE

Recovery after the war

No period in the history of the fishing industry in Shetland can equal the last half century in its cycle of changes, which have brought the islands into the forefront of the industry in the UK.

Traditionally Shetland fishermen had to rely on boats bought second-hand from the north-east of Scotland as fishermen there were taking the next step in the development of their industry. Today Shetland's fleet is as advanced as any in the UK, thanks to the foresight of the fishermen and the guidance of their representatives in Shetland Fishermen's Association.

The Second World War had a devastating effect on the islands' industry as fishermen were called up for war service, while the best of the big boats were

The big Zulu *Fear Not*, white smoke billowing from her exhaust, approaches the quay at Lerwick. She was well looked after during the war, employed in harbour duties at Lerwick and Scalloway, and was given a large roomy wheelhouse.

Photo – Robert Johnson Collection

required by the Admiralty for harbour duties or transport around the UK. Many fishermen were among the 357 Shetlanders who lost their lives in the war and several of the boats that served were sunk or damaged beyond repair. They included the motor boats *Braeflett, Comfort, Honey Dew, Triumph* and *Winsome* and the steam drifters *Lord Dunwich* and *White Daisy*.

With the end of the war in Europe, in May 1945, there was a tremendous urge to get back to normal, to get the boats back to sea, to reopen the traditional markets for herring. Business men in Lerwick were eager to regain the bustle associated with the herring season; but they had to wait a bit longer since the Government was in no hurry to release the boats.

Around 20 small inshore boats took part in the herring fishery in 1945. They included the *Choice, Fern, Homeland, Ivy Lea, Maggie Helen, Passing Cloud, Smiling Morn* and *Swallow*. The only big boats to take part were the *Jeannie, Blossom, Crystal River, Ella II* and *Orcadis*.

They were joined by the *Hawk* and *Roerwater*, two of the many Norwegian fishing boats which had arrived in Shetland during the war carrying refugees. Some of them were bought by Shetland fishermen and usually given new names. The *Roerwater* (skipper John Thomson) opened the season with a fine shot of 94 crans, taken in the Burra Haaf and landed at Scalloway.

Just as the season was about to begin it was realised that the shore-based curing staff had virtually disappeared during the war. The women who had gutted and packed the herring had found a keen demand for knitwear from servicemen based in Shetland, as they sent woollen garments back to their families elsewhere in the UK.

Urgent headlines in the local press, addressed: "To the women of Shetland", asked: "Must the catch go back?" and added: "Women are urgently wanted to help with the herring season."

It was a very short season and the catch was far below the level of pre-war years. Nevertheless it proved to the islands as a whole that life was getting back to normal.

The big boats were back in time for the herring season of 1946, which proved to be highly successful. United Herring Exporters of Lowestoft had obtained a contract from the Civil Control Commission in Germany for a large quantity of herring and had obtained a lease of Alexandra Wharf at Lerwick for their freshing or klondyking operation. These were the names given to the practice – which had started early in the century – of packing ungutted herring in wooden boxes with ice and salt, whereby low temperatures were achieved, and sending them in fast cargo ships to markets in Germany.

The cargo boat *Edina* of Dundee had the honour of taking the first cargo of freshed herring to Germany since 1939. She had to take a devious route to avoid minefields, the journey to Hamburg taking 80 hours instead of the normal 60. Another sign that life was returning to normal was the presence of four English drifters at Lerwick – *Arcady*, *Covent Garden*, *Implacable* and *Golden Miller*.

The local fleet consisted of 50 boats that season, including the big motor boats *Crystal River*, *Fear Not*, *Duthies II*, *Humility*, *Planet*, *Thistle*, *Trust*, *Research* and *Vanguard*. It also included two of the last remaining steam drifters, *The Maid of Thule* and *Girl Lizzie*, under their new names *Clingswater* and *Gossawater*. Earlier that year Thomas Sinclair had sold his drifter the *Friendly Girls* and another survivor, the *Lord Curzon*, was doing salvage work.

There were still fishermen who regarded the steam drifter as the ideal vessel for herring fishing and a crew from Burra, led by Geordie Hunter, brought the *Girl Eileen* to Shetland.

Klondyking operations at Lerwick in 1946, the herring being packed in wooden boxes with ice and salt and transported as quickly as possible to Germany.

Photo – Robert Johnson Collection

The reappraisal

During the war Shetland's fishing fleet had consisted of small Zulus and Fifies and locally built boats of Shetland model design from 35ft to 45ft long, fully decked and with engines up to 30hp. They were crewed by men exempt

The Whalsay boat *Research*, a successful vessel in the early post-war period.

Photo – Shetland Museum

from war service because of age or other factors. They had fished inshore waters, mainly for haddock and whiting, while in the summer they had laid on drift nets for herring fishing.

There was a keen demand during the war years from merchants who supplied major customers on the Scottish mainland and within the islands. Local demand was enhanced by the presence of more than 20,000 servicemen, who defended the islands against possible invasion by German forces stationed in Norway, the nearest point being just 200 miles away.

The small inshore boats must be given credit for developing a new fishing technique as far as Shetland is concerned. In 1926 several boats had winches installed, belt-driven from the fore-end of the engine, to equip them for the Danish form of anchor seining to catch plaice. This was a short lived fishery since the stocks of plaice were found to be limited.

The main breakthrough for this class of boat came in 1940 when they adopted the Scottish form of seining, in which a net with two wings to herd the fish into the bag or codend, is towed by long warps until it closes when the ropes are winched in and the net hauled onboard.

Within a few years the more labour intensive haddock line fishery, for long the mainstay of this class of vessel, was almost extinct. It still had its adherents, who continued to set their baited lines, complaining all the time that their fishery was being destroyed by the seine net.

While the inshore boats could fish economically throughout the year, the big Fifies and Zulus, built as sailing luggers and smacks at the beginning of the century, then having engines installed between the wars, were used solely for herring fishing. Fitted out in April or May, most of them fished for only three or four months, then spent the rest of the year swinging at their anchors in some sheltered voe. Some fishermen actually had two boats — the big herring boat for summer herring fishing and a small more manoeuvrable haddock boat for line fishing during the winter.

The situation had changed with the introduction of seine netting, which gave the potential for year round fishing in one vessel. Fishermen realised that

Part of the Burra haddock line fleet at Hamnavoe just before the Second World War. From the left are: *Be Ready, Ocean's Gift, Homeland, Smiling Morn, Water Lily* and *Sylvanus*. All of them had seine net winches installed after the war.

Photo – John H. Goodlad

it was not cost-effective to have boats which lay idle for the greater part of the year.

It was clear that the future of the fishing industry lay in dual-purpose vessels, able to fish with driftnets for herring in summer and with seine nets for white fish during the rest of the year. The small boats were already doing so, but being unable to carry a sufficient number of herring nets they were about to make seining a year-round activity.

The first steps to efficient dual-purpose fishing were taken at the end of the war when the strongest of the old boats, like the *Banffshire, Research, Planet* and *Duthies II*, had seine net winches installed. These also served as a capstan, the older device that hauled the bush rope to which the herring nets were attached.

The small boats did have one advantage over the big boats in that they were permitted to fish with seine nets on inshore grounds from which large vessels were banned by law.

To legalise fishing for plaice the Fishery Board for Scotland had introduced, in 1926, a by-law (No 41) which allowed anchor seining to be carried out by small vessels with a keel length under 40 feet within three miles of the shore, between the times of sunrise and sunset at Greenwich. In most parts of the country this area was closed to both trawling and seining by vessels of all sizes.

Under this ruling the Scottish type of seine net fishing, often referred to as fly-dragging, was also illegal within three miles of the shore – until the crew of the Lerwick boat *Flower* blew a great hole in this legislation.

Skipper John Duthie appeared in Lerwick Sheriff Court in July 1940, following complaints that he had been fishing with a seine net within the three-mile limit in Sandwick Bay. He was charged with using: "by trawling or dragging along the bottom of the sea", a seine net for the capture of sea fish other than herrings, sprats, sparlings and shellfish, contrary to by-laws made by the Fishery Board for Scotland in 1898.

Skipper Duthie pled not guilty. He pointed out that this type of gear was not a seine net, but a special "haddock net" which had floats along the headline to keep it off the bottom. He claimed that he was merely responding to a plea made on the radio, by the Minister of Food Lord Woolton, that fishermen should use the best method of fishing to bring more fish ashore, to use their own initiative and not wait for orders.

Evidence that the net had indeed been towed along the bottom came from Fishery Officer Andrew Anderson, who pointed out that the *Flower* had landed appreciable quantities of flatfish, which are found only on the seabed.

In spite of a lengthy submission from Mr Anderson, the Sheriff ruled that the prosecution had failed to prove that on this occasion the net was dragged or trawled along the bottom. He found the charge against the accused not proven.

This cleared the way for greater effort by small boats within the three-mile limit as the Fishery Board issued another by-law (No 45). This permitted the use of a Scottish type of seine net within three miles of the Shetland coastline by boats under 50ft long, except within one half mile of the mouth of any stream and not between the hours of sunset and sunrise at Greenwich.

There was plenty of fish around Shetland in the 1940s, partly because the steam trawlers from Aberdeen and other ports, which used to fish extensively around Shetland, often ignoring the three-mile limit, had been diverted to other jobs, such as mine-sweeping, during the war.

An indication of how prolific the inshore grounds were at that time was seen at Scalloway at the end of January 1946, when in one day 17 small seine netters landed 48 tons or 960 boxes of fish. One of the smallest, the 40ft long *Ocean's Gift*, powered by a 25hp engine, had her hold entirely full with 119 boxes.

There was consternation among the fishermen when it was realised that by-law number 45 had expired in April 1943 and many boats had been breaking the law unwittingly by fishing within the three-mile limit at times. This was rectified hurriedly on 20th May, 1946, when the Secretary of State for Scotland approved by-law number 48, which made seining legal within three miles of the shore, subject to the same conditions as before. It was stated that the by-law would remain in force for five years.

The fishing communities

While at one time most communities in Shetland combined crofting with fishing to make a living, the industry that developed after the war demanded a greater degree of commitment. Boats working throughout the year also required piers and other facilities; but these were lacking in most areas.

The main exception was Lerwick where the harbour trust had built a large quay and auction mart for the herring industry in the early part of the century. It had also provided a harbour for small fishing boats near the south end of the town.

Lerwick had a fairly large fishing community, mostly descendants of "immigrants" from towns and villages in north-east Scotland, who had arrived in Shetland from the end of the 19th century, driven north because of overfishing on their home grounds by steam trawlers.

These families had their homes at the north end of Lerwick and their small motor boats were usually berthed in privately owned docks at Freefield and Garthspool. Prominent among them were brothers John and Robert Duthie, who were among the first to take up seine netting as an alternative to fishing with haddock lines.

Lerwick had excellent repair facilities at the Malakoff slipway and there were engineering firms, including Smith and Gair, who specialised in the repair of marine engines and was agent for Kelvin engines. Lerwick also had fish salesmen who auctioned the catches and acted as agents for fishing vessels. The most important of these was LHD Ltd.

An important feature in the north harbour was the scores of herring curing yards, each with its own wooden jetty, which lined the harbour front with an overspill on the Bressay shore. These stations had been lying dormant during the war.

While Lerwick was the main centre in Shetland for the summer herring fishery, Scalloway on the opposite side of Shetland had become the main base for the winter haddock fishery. There were several fish houses, where fish which had been gutted at sea was packed with ice in wooden boxes and dispatched by the North of Scotland Company's steamers to parent firms or customers in Aberdeen, Leith and Glasgow. Scalloway was also the main centre in Shetland for kippering herring with five kilns still usable at the end of the war.

Several fishing families resided in Scalloway, among them those of brothers Joe and Jeemie Alex Watt, who had moved from Crovie in north-east Scotland and married local girls. A prominent herring skipper in the 1940s was Lowrie Ward, skipper of the big Zulu *Fear Not*.

The village had derived a bonus during the war with the building of the Prince Olav Slipway, built by Norwegian engineers to repair the boats of the Shetland Bus operation, which carried out secret missions to occupied Norway. The slipway was operated after the war by William Moore & Son, the local agent for Gardner engines. For a few years a second slipway was in operation at Blacksness, having been constructed for the Royal Air Force which had two fast rescue launches based at Scalloway during the war.

Scalloway had a large quay owned by Blacksness Pier Trust, but it provided little shelter and during bad weather local boats had to depend on moorings laid in the harbour. The inadequacies of Blacksness Pier were highlighted in January 1946 when three boats were badly damaged during a storm.

More than half the fishermen in Shetland were based in the islands of Burra and Whalsay. Burra is blessed with a number of sheltered voes, providing safe anchorages from most wind directions. While the big herring boats spent the winter at anchor off Bridge End or Easter Dale, year round fishing was carried out from Hamnavoe, the main village in the island, the crews landing their catches of haddock and whiting at Scalloway.

Whalsay, on the east side of Shetland, had enormous problems since the main anchorages in the north and south voes of Symbister were exposed to westerly and north-westerly gales. As at Burra the men had to start a fishing trip by rowing off from the beach in a small boat, which then lay at the big boat's moorings waiting for the men to return after landing their catches. Wooden jetties served as landing stages at both Hamnavoe and Symbister.

Whalsay's near neighbour, the island group of Out Skerries, has long been dependent on fishing, having the advantage of a fine natural harbour. Further north the island of Yell has some excellent harbours and here too men returning from the forces were considering the purchase of fishing vessels. Cullivoe led the way with the small seine netters *Rely* and *Reliance* which started the revival in the north of the island.

At the south end of Shetland several families in Dunrossness still had an interest in fishing, with shares in fishing boats or in their fleets of driftnets. The *Laurel*, the last survivor of a once sizeable fleet of sail and motor drifters, fished for several years after the war.

Here a new force in the industry, George W. B. Leslie, was making plans for a big investment in fishing vessels. A member of a land-owning family, he had worked as a building contractor during the war. His first acquisition was the *Duen*, a small Norwegian fishing vessel which with its complement of refugees had made landfall not far from his house.

Mr Leslie had attracted attention before the war with his experiments in locating herring shoals from an aeroplane, by searching for signs which might indicate suitable sea conditions, such as the colouring of the water due to its plankton content. He would drop messages in bottles beside the herring boats as they proceeded to the grounds.

Outside the main fishing areas, often in remote hamlets, men returning from the forces realised that the fishing industry offered opportunities and were preparing to invest their savings in small vessels.

The need for better harbours throughout Shetland created a great deal of discussion at meetings of Zetland County Council during much of 1945. In March the council drew up a plan to ensure that each island had a pier big enough to meet transport needs and encourage fishing.

Sites listed included Fair Isle, Bressay, Whalsay, Skerries, Yell and Unst. These proposals led to controversy as to the most suitable site. This was most marked in Whalsay where a fierce debate developed between those who advocated a site in South Voe and those who preferred North Voe. In Yell there was pressure that Ulsta should be chosen in preference to Mid Yell.

Lerwick Harbour Trust had promoted an ambitious scheme in 1939 and although it had received Government approval its plans had to be shelved until after the war.

Each scheme depended on grant assistance from the Government and those promoting the projects realised that there was likely to be a long wait until funds became available.

The fleet expands

The first post-war addition to Shetland's fishing fleet was the *Swiftwing II*, bought in January 1946 from Fraserburgh by Alex Watt of Lerwick and his sons James and William. She was a sturdy vessel 52 feet long and equipped for both seine netting and drift netting. An interesting piece of equipment was her Marconi Sea Graph echometer – the first in Shetland.

In May that year the small seine net and line fishing boat *Pilot Us* arrived from Fraserburgh for a Whiteness crew (skipper John J. Smith) and Sinclair Cumming of Lerwick purchased the *Betsy Sinclair* from owners in Peterhead.

Later that year John Wiseman of Lerwick bought the *Argo* from Bridlington and renamed her *Girl May II* while George Watt of Lerwick brought the *Excelsior* north from Fraserburgh. In December another small boat arrived for Whiteness, the *Flower* bought from Banff by Charlie Hunter and partners, while another Banff boat the *Foxglove* was bought by George Cogle of Cunningsburgh. The *Pilot Us* had only a brief stay in Whiteness, being bought by Jeemie Alex Watt of Scalloway.

A major factor in the development of the fishing industry throughout the UK was the Inshore Fishing Industry Act of 1945, which provided financial assistance for the building of vessels up to 70 feet long and the renewal of older vessels and engines. Assistance, when approved, came in the form of a grant and a loan – up to 30 per cent in each case.

Another important factor was the availability of a class of vessel known as

Swiftwing II, shown here rigged for herring fishing, after she was sold to Skerries.

Photo – Colin Hughson

7

MFVs – Motor Fishing Vessels. These had been built for the Admiralty during the war, maintaining employment in a number of yards which had produced fishing boats before the war. While intended primarily for a variety of harbour duties they were designed with fishing in mind whenever peace should come. It was a wise move – not typical of decisions taken at a time when the top priority for most people was to win the war at all costs.

The MFVs came in a range of sizes – 50 feet, 60 feet, 75 feet and 90 feet. The 75ft long class was the most popular in Shetland. When bought these vessels still had large deckhouses which were usually replaced fairly quickly with less cumbersome structures when more finance became available. Before starting their new careers their holds were fitted out for carrying fish and a seine net winch was installed on deck. The first of these to arrive in Shetland was the *Margaret Reid*, bought by George Leslie in 1946.

Margaret Reid, an MFV acquired by George Leslie soon after the war.

Photo – Robert Johnson Collection

A problem for some fishermen was the qualifications now required before taking command of a large vessel. A skipper now had to have a Second Hand Special certificate, which required a period of study followed by an examination. Classes organised by the Further Education department of Shetland Education Committee were held in several places. At Lerwick they were conducted by Tom Moncrieff, at Scalloway by David Howarth and Hance Smith, at Burra by Captain John R. Duncan and at Whalsay by Captain Thomas Shearer.

Some skippers discovered to their surprise and disappointment that they were slightly colour blind; and in spite of having a lifetime's experience of fishing and navigation, they had to give command of their vessel to a younger crewmember who had passed the exam.

One of the most far seeing people in Shetland at this time was a Lerwick shopkeeper James G. Peterson, better known as Pete. In 1946 he advocated a boat building venture which would produce a range of boats designed specifically for the needs of Shetland fishermen, to be built within the islands.

His comments attracted the attention of David Howarth, who as Lt. Commander Howarth had been attached to the Norwegian wartime base at Scalloway. Mr Howarth offered to design a boat suitable for Shetland and to start a boatbuilding business at Scalloway if a crew could be found willing to invest in such a vessel. It was expected that it would cost around £6000 and few fishermen had the means to undertake such a commitment at that time.

Mr Peterson agreed to put up half the sum and he found a partnership in Burra, with skipper John William Pottinger of Whiteness, willing to raise the other half. They had applied for grant assistance but had been turned down.

The result was the *Enterprise*, launched on 22nd March, 1947. She was a lovely vessel with the raking stem of a Shetland model and a cruiser stern. She was powered by a 120hp Wichmann engine imported specially from Norway, driving a variable pitch propeller. By this time Shetland fishermen had realised that a diesel engine was more reliable and economical than the old-fashioned petrol/paraffin engines.

The Scalloway-built *Enterprise*, seen here in Aberdeen.

Photo – Shetland Museum

On her first night at sea at the start of the summer herring fishery, the *Enterprise* had a shot of 30 crans. It was a good omen since she was a successful vessel throughout her career. She was also the fastest boat in the Scottish fleet at the time with a speed of just under 10 knots.

After the *Enterprise* Howarth's yard produced the 50 ft long *Endeavour* for a Whiteness crew, the slightly smaller *Bonnie Isle* for a crew in Whalsay and the *Northern Ranger* for a Scalloway crew. Two orders from Caithness resulted in the building of the *Golden Eagle* and *Maid of Honour*. Then the yard encountered financial problems and it closed in 1952.

The flow of good second-hand boats continued. A further two MFVs for Lerwick were the *Mary Watt* and *John West* while the *Jessie Sinclair* was bought by Bob Williamson and partners of Burra. George Leslie bought a second MFV which he named *Jean Leslie*. She was later sold to owners in Burra and renamed *Cornucopia* (skipper Lowrie Goodlad).

A large number of sturdy old Fifies and Zulus were bought by fishermen in Burra. They included the *Fleetwing* owned by Jeemie and Scott Gray, the *Sunshine* (Scott Ward), *Fisher Lassie* (Raymie Laurenson), *Harmonious*,

9

The 50ft long *Endeavour* arriving at Lerwick with 114 crans of herring.

Photo – Robert Johnson Collection

renamed *Easter Rose* (J. R. Christie), *Golden West* (Stewart Jamieson) and *Maid of the Mist* (James S. Inkster). The *Surprise*, formerly a Scalloway boat, was brought back from Eyemouth by Andrew Halcrow, a merchant in Hamnavoe, and John Henry, a butcher in Lerwick, and began fishing with Arthur Pottinger as skipper. The seine netter *Sea Gleaner* (Joe Watt) was added to the Scalloway fleet and the *Budding Rose* (George L. Smith) began fishing from Whiteness.

The inshore fleet at Lerwick expanded with the addition of the *Mayflower* (James Wiseman), *Launch Out* (Alex John Watt), *Harvest Gold* (Robbie Watt) and *Glad Tidings* (Alex Wiseman).

John Duncan of Lerwick sold the *Rely* to Andrew Spence of Cullivoe and replaced her with the bigger boat *Golden Ray*, renamed *Freedom*. Additions to the Skerries fleet, both from Lerwick, were the *Snowdrop* and *Swiftwing II*. The owner of the *Snowdrop*, Thomas Hutchison and partners, had a Bendix echosounder installed.

Some crews found boats in Shetland suitable for renovation. The old sailboat *Lord Roberts* was converted into the motor boat *Northern Light* by Robbie Pottinger and partners of Burra, while the Tait family of Burra had the old line fishing boat *Kate* restored as the *Sunbeam*. They later sold her to John Robert and Joseph Watt of Scalloway and replaced her with the 51ft long *Celerity*.

Henry and Tom Scott Goodlad of Scalloway renovated the *Innovator* (*ex-Majestic*) as the *Norseman's Bride*. John West of Lerwick had the *Kitchener* renovated as the *Blossom* before acquiring the MFV *John West*.

J. & M. Shearer of Lerwick, the most important local herring curing firm after the war, owned three vessels used originally as flit-boats – the *Day Dawn*, *Jeannie* and *Margaret* – which were renovated and leased to fishermen in Whalsay. This was only a temporary move since most fishermen now preferred to own their vessels and were able to do so because of the loans and grants available from the Government.

A new boat acquired in 1948 was the 50ft long *Young Dawn*, built by James Noble of Fraserburgh for Sinclair Cumming and partners of Lerwick. Also in that year the *Foxglove*, renamed *Flowing Tide*, was purchased by David Anderson and partners of Mid Yell.

Another new boat the *Harvest Hope* arrived in March 1949 for Alex and Robert Duthie of Lerwick. Built by Stephens of Banff, she was 57ft long and was powered by a 114 hp Gardner engine. A few months later the 58ft long *Mary Jane* powered by a 96hp Gardner engine, was bought second-hand by Laurence Irvine and partners of Whalsay and the ring netter *Endeavour* was bought by J. W. Hughson and partners of Skerries and renamed *Triumph*.

There was also an interesting development in Unst where Duncan Mouat of Haroldswick acquired the *Village Maid*. A few months earlier George Inkster of Baltasound had begun fishing with the seine netter *Desire*.

The *Betty Leslie*, the biggest boat in Shetland in the early post-war period.

Photo – Shetland Museum

Another new boat towards the end of 1949 was the 52ft long *Ocean Star* for James and George Watt of Lerwick, while the 70ft long *Summer Rose* was built by Jones of Buckie for John and James Watt. She was powered by a 160 hp Gleniffer engine. The largest boat to arrive that year was the *Betty Leslie*, a 90ft long MFV acquired by George Leslie of Sumburgh. She was to have an outstanding career in Shetland and was chosen for an experiment which could have altered the pattern of herring fishing in the UK. In 1950 she had a Norwegian purse seine installed 250 fathoms long and 50 fathoms deep. Modifications to the vessel, carried out at St Monans, included the fitting of a "turntable" nine feet square at the stern of the vessel for laying the net, which had rings along the footrope through which a steel wire could perform the pursing operation. It was shot only once when lack of experience led to the net being torn on hard bottom and the experiment came to a premature end. Nethertheless the *Betty Leslie* could claim to be Britain's first purse seiner.

The high point of 1950 was the arrival of three boats, all around 70 feet long, for owners in Hamnavoe — the *Dauntless* (Alex John Henry), *Press On* (James Henry) and *Replenish* (John L. Pottinger). They arrived in time for the herring season, the *Replenish* missing part of it.

As a result of all these additions to the fleet Manson's Shetland Almanac for 1951, showing the strength of the fleet the previous year, included three steam drifters, 70 first class motor boats and 75 second class boats (generally boats with a keel length from 18 to 35 feet). Some of the latter were inshore seine netters while others worked lines or cod nets or were used part-time fishing for lobsters, a new fishery which was growing in importance.

Burra led the way with a fleet of 25 first class boats while 23 were based at Lerwick. Each of these places had 13 second class vessels. Eight first class boats and seven second class vessels were based at Whalsay, indicating the extent to which the island was hampered by the lack of a safe harbour.

A new routine

In spite of so many additions to Shetland's fishing fleet, it still consisted mainly of old Zulus and Fifies built in the early part of the century and given a new lease of life after having seine net gear installed.

The Whiteness seine netter *Budding Rose*. She has just started to tow; while a crewmember stows the dhan for'ard and the ropes are tightening astern.

Photo – Magnus Sinclair

The crews adapted quickly to the new routine. Arriving on the grounds the skipper had to select an area where there was normally a good stock of fish at that time of year. He also had to make sure from his experience of the area that there were no seabed obstructions – referred to as fasteners – in which the gear might become entangled. These included pinnacles of rock, wrecks going back hundreds of years and even aircraft, lost during the recent war.

First the dhan was thrown overboard and attached to it was one end of the first side of rope. The boat got under way, paying out the first four or five coils of rope, before turning to make the loop which would form the base of the fishing triangle.

Then the boat slowed down while a wing of the seine net was clipped on to the end of the rope, the netting being thrown out from the stern of the vessel to ensure that it did not become entangled in the rudder or propeller. The first wing was followed by the bag of the net and then the second wing, to which the end of the ropes lying coiled on the other side of the vessel was now attached.

After shooting more rope to complete the base of the triangle the boat turned and headed back to the dhan. On misty days it might not be easy to locate the dhan, in spite of the coloured flag attached to its stalk.

The ends of both sides of the warps were secured to the drums of the winch which was set in motion in low gear and the boat began to tow the net. The two lines of rope actually guided the fish within the triangle towards the net where the steadily closing wings herded them into the bag. The winch was put into low gear and the ropes were pulled in, running in cages one on either quarter.

When the two lengths of rope were lying almost parallel to each other over the stern of the boat the skipper knew that the net was closed. The winch was now put in top gear to haul the net as quickly as possible, the ropes being coiled by a 'coiler' then stowed on deck by hand.

Seabirds were usually the first to spot the net as it approached the surface and if there was a good catch the bag would often rise to the surface some distance astern of the boat. In the early days of this operation the catch was lifted onboard by hand. Usually there was too much fish to be taken onboard in one lift and the bag would be left floating alongside the boat and only the codend hauled onboard with part of the catch. The knot securing the end of the codend would be untied to let the fish cascade into pounds or wooden boxes placed on deck. The knot would be re-tied and the codend flung back into the sea, being refilled as more of the bag was hauled by hand onto the boat. The Burra boat *Thistle* (John Leask) was the first to have a derrick installed, whereby greater quantities of fish could be taken onboard with each lift by mechanical means.

Occasionally one tow would produce 50 or 60 boxes, providing sufficient work for the crew to gut and wash in one day. But usually the shooting and hauling would continue until late afternoon, when the skipper decided that it was time to head for port to land the catch.

Lifting the catch onboard the Lerwick seine netter *Star Divine*. Those who can be identified are skipper W. G. Nicol (left) and L. Robertson.

Photo – J. Nicol

When the seine net replaced the haddock line it meant longer hours at sea for the fishermen; but for the women who had cleared and baited the lines as part of the daily routine it meant virtual emancipation. They now had more time to look after their houses; the cold draughty baiting sheds were now used as stores; and with greater income from the seine net the women became more house-proud – even to the extent of replacing linoleum with carpets.

The seine net brought dangers to the unwary. The greatest danger lay in the winch, with the seine net ropes winding relentlessly round the drums. In those days fishermen wore long oilskin coats which, if one came too close, could be caught between the rope and the drum.

An accident on the Scalloway boat *Britannia*, when Archibald and John Fullerton sustained multiple injuries, emphasised the dangers involved. On a big Zulu or Fifie there was more space on deck for stowing the ropes as they came off the winch; but in a small boat like the *Britannia* space was limited and the rotating winch a serious threat.

Another danger arose when the rope was being shot. Sometimes a circle of rope would get out of place, being looped behind another one with the result that a tangle of rope was heading for the shooting pole – a device with a roller stuck in the rail, its aim to keep the rope for'ard of the area where the men were gutting the catch. On such an occasion it was easy to get a loop of rope around one's ankle, with the danger of being hauled overboard.

Although the big new boats had a galley in the deckhouse, the crew still ate and slept in the cabin aft or, in the case of the smaller boats, a cramped fo'c'sle. An innovation in the bigger boats was the toilet at the after end of the deckhouse – a cubicle with a wooden seat and a bucket which was emptied after use.

For many crews the high point of the year was the herring fishing. At the end of April or the beginning of May the seine net gear was put ashore; the hold was rearranged for carrying herring; the thick tarry bush rope was hauled onboard from a quayside store; and finally the driftnets, dry and dusty after being kept in a dry shed or loft over the winter, were carried on board and the canvas bowes that provided flotation for the fleet of driftnets were stored in their compartment in the hold.

There were still a few boats like the *Fear Not* and *Crystal River* which spent the winter lying at anchor. For them preparations were more extensive, as they had to be put on the slip to have the winter's growth of weed removed and the engines had to be overhauled.

There was still a lingering fondness for the winter herring fishing as a few boats fitted out in January and struggled to make a living in wintry seas as far north as the north end of Unst. Those involved in the early post-war years were the *Gossawater*, *Thistle*, *Blossom*, *Mary Watt* and *Cornucopia*. The herring they caught were part of the Atlanto-Scandian stock.

Some boats, after a short break at the end of the summer herring season, would go to fish at East Anglia. The Shetland contingent in 1946 included the *Gossawater*, *Clingswater*, *Margaret Reid*, *Blossom* and *Humility*, while the following year the Shetland boats *Margaret Reid*, *Mary Watt*, *Jean Leslie*, *Clingswater* and *Margaret* made the long journey south. In 1948 six boats went to fish off East Anglia – the *Cornucopia*, *Mary Watt*, *Girl Eileen*, *Gossawater*, *Humility* and *Betty Leslie*. It was not a happy trip for the *Cornucopia* which was in collision with the iron drifter *Convallaria* and spent two weeks being repaired.

Ten boats went south in 1949 – the steam drifters *Girl Eileen* and *Gossawater*, the MFVs *Betty Leslie*, *Mary Watt*, *Margaret Reid*, *Cornucopia*, *Jessie Sinclair* and *John West*, the old vessels *Humility* and *Northern Light* and the new boat *Summer Rose*.

The *Betty Leslie* had the biggest catch of the season and went to Ijmuiden with 256¾ crans to earn over £1000 for her night's work. Had she landed her catch at East Anglia she would have won the Prunier Trophy that year.

Most of the smaller boats stayed with the seine net fishing throughout the year, apart from those like the *Pilot Us* of Scalloway which fished with lines for halibut during the summer. Several boats fished with gill nets for cod in the early part of the year.

The small seine netters found the winter particularly hard and many crews from Burra, Scalloway and Lerwick found it far more pleasant to work in St Magnus Bay for months at a time, landing their catches at Voe.

The start of a new technology

The introduction of the echosounder was hailed as the miracle of the age since for the first time it gave fishermen "eyes" under the sea. It had been developed between the wars as an aid to navigation, by showing the depth of water under a vessel. Echoes of sound waves "bounced" off the seabed and the time interval between transmission and reception was registered automatically as a continuous graph in the recording instrument in the ship's wheelhouse.

Sometimes an echo was recorded between the vessel and the seabed and fishermen realised that these were echoes from shoals of fish. Suddenly the echosounder achieved an importance which those who developed this technique had not intended.

No one was more interested in this application than George Leslie who before the war had put so much effort into spotting the signs of herring shoals from the air. The experiment was repeated once after the war when Mr Leslie chartered a plane from Sumburgh and, having seen a promising area south of Sumburgh Head, gave instructions to the crew of the *Duen* as to where they should shoot their nets. Unfortunately when the *Duen* arrived in the area the promising signs were no longer there.

With the introduction of the echosounder herring spotting became a more exact science. Fishermen still looked for the tell-tale signs that suggested that herring could be in the area – whales blowing, seabirds diving or a milky appearance in the water denoting plenty of plankton – but unless there were "marks" on the echosounder it was unlikely that the vessel would shoot its nets there.

When the echosounder on the *Margaret Reid* broke down Mr Leslie contacted James Williamson of the Scalloway firm H. Williamson & Sons who managed to repair it. Mr Leslie was so impressed that he wrote to Kelvin Hughes, suggesting that the firm should appoint the Scalloway firm as their agent in Shetland. This started a close involvement with the fishing industry which the firm maintains today.

The echosounder was also useful in identifying types of seabed suitable for the seine net. Hard bottom was indicated by a darker line and the peaks and troughs of a very irregular seabed, which would tear a net to ribbons. In this way large areas around Shetland were found to be suitable for seine-netting, enabling the fishery to develop rapidly in the early post-war period.

The traditional system of locating fishing grounds by landmarks (meids) still continued. In the Burra Haaf an elaborate system had developed over the years whereby fishermen could pinpoint areas of soft or hard bottom with amazing accuracy. Their positions along a north-south line was identified as the steep slope of the north hill of Quarff "moved" along the prominent features in the profile of Burra. Their position on an east-west line was given by the Point of Skeld as it was seen to shift against a background of distant hills.

Another innovation of this period was the radio-telephone, whereby fishermen could keep in touch with their colleagues in different areas and move to wherever the best catches were being obtained. In some cases failure to contact a skipper might be an indication that he was making good catches and did not want any competition.

The trawler band of the radio was popular with the families of fishermen ashore, as for the first time they were able to follow the movements of the boats during the day. Even those with no direct involvement in fishing tuned to the trawler band as often as possible, such was the level of interest in the industry at that time.

This was particularly true during the herring season when hundreds of people all over Shetland listened intently as the skippers discussed marks and the colour of the water. After a few hours sleep some enthusiasts were back at their sets at 3 or 4 am to hear whether the first nets hauled gave the promise of a good catch and they noted what the various boats had at the "half bowe".

Then at 7.40 am as most folk were preparing for their day's work, Robbie Pottinger of the *Northern Light*, on her way ashore, would come on the air "speakin hame" to the families of his crew with the introduction: "Hullo Roseville, Number Four, Braemar, Southerhouse and Hapwell." He would then proceed to list the estimated catches of the entire fleet.

Another popular feature with many people was hymn singing by men like

Harry Laurenson of the *Replenish*, late at night after the nets had been shot. When the theme was taken up by skippers from ports in the north-east of Scotland it was an experience not to be forgotten. Someone said it reminded you of the Sea of Galilee. Such abuse of the airwaves was frowned upon by the authorities and eventually made illegal.

There was an excellent choice of marine radios, produced by four main firms — Coastal of Edinburgh, Marconi of Chelmsford and Woodsons and Telemarine of Aberdeen.

Shetland Fishermen's Association

Despite the long tradition of fishing in Shetland there is no evidence of any organisation or association to represent the interests of local fishermen until the early part of the century.

In 1901 at an open air meeting at Freefield in Lerwick the "Shetland Fishermen's Association" was formed as a reaction to the common practice by herring curers changing their bid for fish after the auction on the grounds that the herring did not match the quality of the sample. This was a common practice when curers realised that heavy catches were coming in and the price would drop during the day. Instrumental in forming this association was local fish salesman James Robertson, who was appointed secretary.

During those early years the association was active in calling for the closure of the Norwegian-owned whaling stations in Shetland which, it was believed, were responsible for the declining herring catches.

This association appears to have lapsed after Mr Robertson went to university in 1910. His brother John W. Robertson became involved in a successor organisation called the Shetland Herring and White Fish Protection Association. It was active until 1930 and was noted for its opposition to the growing effort by trawlers around Shetland.

The Shetland Fishermen's Association is again recorded as being the representative organisation from 1930 to 1936, although it is uncertain how active it may have been. The secretary was John Taylor, headteacher at Hamnavoe. He was succeeded by another Burra man Jeemie Pottinger who carried on the work on a voluntary basis.

Jeemie Pottinger, the strength behind the Association in its early years.

It is probably fair to conclude that those early organisations tended to be established in response to specific problems and so lacked any formal structure or management. The scattered nature of Shetland's main fishing communities would also have made it difficult for fishermen to have regular meetings except during the summer months, when most local vessels were based at Lerwick during the herring season.

During the war Shetland fishermen appear to have lacked any local association and were instead in membership of the Scottish Herring Producers Association and, from 1943, of the Scottish Inshore White Fish Producers Association. It seems that herring fishermen were member of both associations and at times one group could complete a job started by the other.

Immediately after the war it was clear that a large number of fishermen wanted to have a local association. After several meetings it was agreed: "to form an independent Shetland Fishermen's Association to be known as such" on 13th December, 1947. Mr Lowrie Ward moved that both existing branches should be merged into one and this was seconded by John Johnson.

As an amendment William Duncan moved that the Shetland branch of the Scottish Herring Producers Association be continued as before. He was supported by Tammie Alec Goodlad. The amendment was carried by 13 votes to three.

The new Shetland Fishermen's Association differed from most of the pre-war bodies in that it had a permanent secretary in Jeemie Pottinger, who ran the association from his home at Hamnavoe. First chairman was skipper John Thomson. In March 1948 it was accepted as a member of the Federation of Scottish Herring and White Fish Catchers, based at Campbeltown.

John Thomson, appointed as the first chairman of the newly formed Shetland Fishermen's Association in 1947.

CHAPTER TWO

Marketing the catch

During the Second World War the market in Europe for salt herring, the main product of Shetland's fisheries, had been destroyed. Government officials realised that it would take a long time for this to recover, even in a reduced form, and they began to look for other outlets.

Between the wars the demand for frozen fish had risen substantially and it was realised that this process could provide part of the answer to Shetland's problem.

Lerwick was selected by the Herring Industry Board as a suitable place for an experimental factory, equipped with kippering and quick freezing lines. The site chosen was the former Anglo-Scottish curing station at North Ness, used during the war as the base for Norwegian motor torpedo boats. Work went ahead during the spring of 1946 and the factory was ready in time for the summer herring fishery.

The Herring Industry Board also co-operated with Herring By-Products Ltd, the owners of the reduction plant at Heogan at the north end of Bressay. In April 1946 new machinery, including a flame dryer, arrived from Bergen in the fishing vessel *Gullhorn*. Fish meal and oil would be produced at a fixed rate on behalf of the board.

This outlet would take care of herring surplus to market requirements or catches which had deteriorated during long journeys, and remove the loss of income experienced so often in the past, when catches had to be dumped back into the sea.

Herring Industry Board kippers being packed for shipment south.

Photo – Shetland Museum

In 1946 the Board introduced a scheme whereby the entire catch was purchased at flat rates for the various outlets – cured, frozen, kippered and meal and oil – and a bonus was paid at the end of the season, its size dependent on the profits made by the Board, working on behalf of the fishermen in the marketing of the catch. This system, which was known as the "pool", was to remain in force for several years.

Although carried out on a smaller scale than in pre-war years, the 1946 season was the most remunerative ever for those taking part. The 46 local boats involved averaged well over £3000 for the season, including what they received from the "pool".

The catch amounted to 63,000 crans worth £159,000. A total of 24,878 barrels were cured; a further 18,185 barrels were rough packed with ungutted herring and salt; and 23,238 crans were "freshed". Most of the salted and freshed herring were sent direct to Altona and Cuxhaven, to alleviate the food shortage in Germany and Poland.

The freezing plant at the HIB factory handled 1399 crans, this consignment of frozen herring being sent to an outlet in England in a Dutch refrigerated cargo vessel. Only 5964 crans were reduced to meal and oil.

Nine curing stations were in operation that year, seven at Lerwick and one each at Scalloway and Symbister. Scalloway had two kippering kilns in operation and Lerwick one, in addition to the HIB's kippering operation. Together they handled 3416 crans.

J. & M. Shearer's curing yard at Lerwick. The boat being unloaded is the *Research*. A "railway" brings the catch from the quay to the farlins where it will be gutted, prior to salting in barrels.

Photo – Magnus Shearer collection

The post-war herring boom continued in 1948 with a fleet of 120 vessels of which 50 motor boats and three steam drifters belonged to Shetland fishermen. The catch amounted to 142,270 crans valued at £420,997. It seemed to many that Shetland – and Lerwick in particular – was about to regain the importance of pre-war years.

Over 900 fishermen were employed that year, nearly half of them from Shetland. There were 351 gutters of whom 124 were Shetlanders, the rest from Scotland and Ireland. Curing was carried out by 11 firms operating 13 stations. Ten of these were at Lerwick while J. & M. Shearer had resumed operations at Cullivoe as well as Symbister and Laurence Williamson had a small curing business at Scalloway.

The HIB's quick freezing plant at Lerwick handled just over 11,000 crans. It also increased its workforce with a large number of students from colleges and universities in several parts of the UK. This set the pattern for the next few years as the students became part of the summer scene at Lerwick.

Klondyking (freshing) was carried out in a big way at Lerwick as United Herring Exporters Ltd of Lowestoft used both Alexandra Wharf and the breakwater at the small boat harbour to load cargo ships with boxes of herring mixed with ice and salt before sailing for Hamburg, Altona and Cuxhaven. A total of 55,390 crans was dispatched in this way.

Sadly the promise of 1948 was not fulfilled. In 1949, when 50 local boats took part in the fishery and 90 English and Scottish vessels were licensed to come north, only 73,894 crans were landed, valued at £217,000. A few local boats had gross earnings over £4000.

The 1950 season was even worse with 53,518 crans valued at £149,419 while in 1951 the total catch was a mere 31,475 crans worth £92,640.

It is difficult to account for the wide fluctuations in the herring fishery which continued throughout the 1950s. On some occasions erratic ocean currents may have brought cold water to the surface, with unusual species of plankton or no plankton at all, forcing the herring to seek their preferred food elsewhere.

Perhaps the main reason for the failure of the fishery on several occasions was the small size of the fleet compared to pre-war years, being unable to cover the entire sea area around Shetland. If the fleet had been larger and more widespread the chance of some vessel encountering a shoal of herring would have been greater, leading the rest of the fleet to that area on subsequent nights.

The market for white fish

During the war the catches of seine netters and line boats were all landed locally and allocated among the various firms who repacked the fish, already gutted at sea, in shipping boxes with ice at the bottom and top of each box. These boxes had lids which were secured with nails driven through a metal hoop at each end. The boxes were then transferred to Lerwick's Victoria Pier and loaded onto the *St Magnus* or some other vessel operated by the North of Scotland Shipping Company, for shipment to Aberdeen. From there most of the fish was sent by rail to firms in Glasgow, Newhaven and elsewhere.

Scalloway had several fish houses, operated by such firms as W. S. Unkles, Hines Brothers, Roderick Dewar, David Mackenzie and Laurence Williamson, important buyers at Lerwick were Shetland Fish Distributors and J. & M. Shearer. The catch was not sold by auction, the Government having introduced a fixed price scheme early in the war to prevent the price of fish rising to unaffordable levels due to scarcity.

The controlled price in Shetland was generally 45/- a hundredweight (cwt) for haddock and 35/- a cwt for whitings, but merchants generally paid a few pence less to compensate for the extra freight charges on fish sent to markets on the mainland.

This system came to an end in 1950 after pressure from boat owners at the main UK ports, who realised that a return to selling by auction would lead to much higher prices. In Shetland, on the other hand, prices had been higher during the war under the controlled price system and there were fears that under the auction system prices would plummet, because of Shetland's distance from the main markets.

The first post-war auction sale took place at Scalloway on Monday 17th April, 1950, in the late afternoon – the first for nine years. 25 boats landed 270 boxes, the *Harvest Hope* having the top shot of 38 boxes. The sale started at 5pm, being conducted by Allie Gear and Bertie Robertson with assistance from LHD's Scalloway based employee Walter Duncan. To the surprise of everyone present haddock sold for 61/- to 68/- a cwt and whiting 42/- to 49/- per cwt.

No one expected those high prices to continue and soon quayside prices at Lerwick and Scalloway were again below the level of those elsewhere in the UK. As the number of seine netters increased steadily conventional markets proved inadequate. While fishermen on the west side of Shetland and those based at Lerwick had the benefit of a daily market, those in Whalsay had no such provision and they began to consign their catches to agents in Aberdeen, who sold the fish in the market on their behalf. Some had been doing this during the war.

The first boat to do so post-war may have been the *Jeannie* which in October 1945 attracted the attention of the local media. It was reported that the crew had fished for two or three days, gutting and packing their catch in the hold, then heading for Lerwick where the catch was transferred to the *St Magnus*, "without being handled ashore".

The innovation which made this possible was the new ice plant at Lerwick started by J. & M. Shearer, producing 1 ton of ice per hour in 1 cwt blocks, which were crushed and bagged and sold at Lerwick for £2 per ton. Boats which landed their catches daily at Lerwick and Scalloway did not use ice at that time.

An important outlet on the east side of Shetland was the Scottish Co-operative Wholesale Society (SCWS) which had the ex-fishing boat *Equity I* running between Lerwick and Peterhead with cargoes of fresh fish. The company extended this service to Whalsay when it had the old steam drifter *Helen Slater* anchored in the North Voe. It was intended that she should be a floating depot, manned by a crew of four, to pack the catches of local fishermen for shipment by the *Equity I*, which would call twice a week.

The project had an unfortunate start since during the *Helen Slater*'s first night at anchor a severe storm caused her to drag her anchor and she drove down on the *Day Dawn*, causing a considerable amount of damage. The crew of the *Helen Slater* learned to cope with the extremes of weather in the North Voe and the vessel became a valuable outlet for fishermen in both Whalsay and Skerries.

As the fleet of seine netters continued to grow and catches increased, prices at local markets began to tumble and more boats began to consign their fish to Aberdeen. It involved a greater effort than "landing on the pier" but the higher prices obtained at Aberdeen generally compensated for the extra labour.

Each boat had to acquire a few hundred shipping boxes, marked with the name and registration number of the vessel. There was a constant need for replacement as many boxes got damaged during loading and unloading by the dockers. The boxes were stacked six high in double tiers within iron chains which, when lifted by the ship's crane, bit into the sides of the upper boxes, causing damage to the sides and lids. The fishermen also had to pay freight charges and handling charges incurred by the agents at Aberdeen, followed by more freight charges as the empty boxes were returned to Shetland.

It is not surprising that some crews decided that it would be far more convenient to fish for three or four days, boxing the catch with ice in the hold, and then head for Aberdeen. This system became known as tripping.

At Aberdeen there were strict rules and regulations laid down by the harbour authority and there were strict rules laid down by the dockers' union. Boats with catches of less than 120 cwt were allowed to land their catches in the seine net berth, at the top of the market; but those which had a full hold had to employ "lumpers" to unload the catch, paying them a handsome fee for doing so.

The Burra boat *Sunshine II* leaving Ronas Voe and heading for the fishing grounds.

Photo – Jim Henry

By September 1950 tripping was a common practice among the bigger boats in the fleet which could expect to obtain gross earnings of £450 to £500 for a week's catch.

The smaller seine netters, too small to "run the market" and with space onboard for only one or two days' catches, had no option but to land their catches at local markets. There were several occasions, when catches were heavy, that local outlets could not absorb their catches and the boats had to stay in port until the demand improved.

There was therefore much excitement when, in the autumn of 1950, the Herring Industry Board leased its processing plant at Lerwick to a major processor Macfisheries, trading as Fromac, to fillet and freeze large quantities of haddock and whiting during the winter and spring.

The fleet expands

The expansion seen in the post-war years continued throughout the 1950s. Arrivals in 1951 included the 51ft long *Fair Dawn*, brought north from Banff by James Hutchison of Whalsay, and the 60ft long *Prossum*, bought by John Leask of Lerwick. She was renamed *Wave Sheaf*.

Early in 1952 the *Pathfinder* and *Silver Cloud* joined the Scalloway fleet when bought by brothers Henry and Tom Scott Goodlad, while in November that year their father Tammy Alec. Goodlad bought the 65ft long *Golden Lily* from owners in St Monans. Built in 1938 she had a 100hp National engine. Another boat for Scalloway that year was the *Godetia* (Jocky Stewart) while additions to the Whalsay fleet were the *Liberty* (John Irvine) and *Our Queen* (Willie Anderson).

In 1953 the 50ft *Nil Desperandum* was bought by Jeemie Wiseman of Lerwick. The following year the 57ft long *Lilac* arrived at Whalsay for skipper Davie Anderson while the *Responsive*, a 65ft long MFV, joined the Lerwick fleet under skipper Robert Duthie. Two years later she was bought by skipper Willie Goodlad and partners of Scalloway. In October 1954 the *Margarita* arrived from Fraserburgh for James Watt of Lerwick and another two boats arrived for Burra – the *Brighter Dawn* (Walter Inkster) and

Southern Cross (Ertie Fullerton). The latter was a 75ft long MFV built at Peterhead in 1946.

Two boats that joined the Whalsay fleet in 1955 were the *Golden Acres* (R. J. Williamson) and *Serene*, a 70ft long vessel built for skipper Mackie Polson and partners. Additions to the Burra fleet that year were the 70ft long *Golden Harvest* (Jeemie Fullerton) and the 72ft long *Sunshine II* (Jeck Ward). A third boat for Burra in 1955 was the Aberdeen registered *Arran Corrie*, a 75ft long MFV bought by skipper Geordie Hunter and partners. She was renamed *Ocean Reaper*. An important addition to the small fleet at Cullivoe was the 50ft long Zulu *St Vincent* built by Andrew Spence and partners.

The 50ft long seine netter *St Vincent* based at Cullivoe.

Photo – Robert Johnson

In March 1956 the *Winner* arrived at Scalloway for skipper Norman Henry and another MFV the *Scotch Queen* joined the Burra fleet for skipper Raymie Laurenson. The following year no less than five boats joined the Whalsay fleet – *Brighter Morn* (R. J. Hutchison), *Orion* (Samuel Irvine), *Xmas Rose* (James G. Leask), *La Morlaye* (Johnnie Jamieson) and *Unity* (James Hutchison).

In 1958 another two boats arrived at Hamnavoe – the *Venture* (Jeemie Cumming) and *Sceptre* (Tommy Fullerton). Other additions to the island's fleet were the 50ft long *Still Waters* bought by James S. Inkster and partners and the *Wave Sheaf* purchased from John Leask by Jeemsie Ward and partners. More additions for Whalsay were the *Planet*, built for skipper Willie Anderson, the *Fortuna* for skipper Jeemie Stewart, the *Comrades* (Tammie Hutchison) and the *Verdant* (Willie Irvine).

The 1950s saw the scrapping of many of the old herring boats which had served Shetland well for nearly half a century. The last of the steam drifters, the *Gossawater*, completed her last season in 1952 and was sold for salvage work. She ended her career in style by catching 287 crans on her last night at the herring fishing.

In 1953 around 30 old Zulus and Fifies took part in the summer herring fishery but by 1955 their numbers were down to 14. In 1956 only eight of those veterans were left – the *Blossom, Day Dawn, Joey Brown, Northern Light, Research, Reaper, Speedwell* and *Swan*. Most of the others had been hauled ashore and broken up to make fencing posts for Shetland's crofters. In

The steam drifter *Gossawater* low in the water with 260 crans. This was her last season and she was Shetland's last steam drifter.

Photo – Dennis Coutts

1958 the *Research* was the last survivor of her class and still one of the most successful vessels in the herring fleet.

Some of the smaller vessels were sold for conversion into cabin cruisers. This was the fate of the *Foxglove*, *Rely* and *Victory*, while the *Triumph* was converted into the Yell Sound ferry *Shalder*. The *Surprise*, having been sold and renamed *Morning Star*, sank after striking a rock on the east coast of Burra. She was refloated and renamed *Hirta II*, serving as a ferry running between Scalloway and Hamnavoe and also operating cruises for summer visitors. The *Budding Rose* from Burra started a new career as a pilot boat with Lerwick Harbour Trust and the *Reaper* was bought by Zetland County Council as a small cargo vessel.

As the herring fishing became more uncertain, the number of boats taking part in it dropped steadily until by the late 1950s only 20 crews considered the effort worthwhile. The others preferred the opportunity to make a regular income from seine netting throughout the year.

For some crews, however, the herring fishery was still the high point of the year, its uncertainty being one of its attractions, with the possibility that the coming season might prove highly successful.

Klondyking stopped in 1953. The Baltic states that formed part of the Communist bloc regarded the development of the fishing industry as the main plank in their economic strategy and within a few years their drifters and trawlers could catch practically all the herring they required.

In the early 1950s East European vessels appeared around Shetland in large numbers. This was the peak of the cold war and their presence created a great deal of speculation in the British media as to their real motives for coming here.

In Shetland however mistrust soon gave way to acceptance and even friendship, as these vessels began to use Basta Voe in Yell and other bays in the North Isles as anchorages in bad weather, while water tankers called regularly at Lerwick as they ran a shuttle service to the fishing vessels and mother ships. Some vessels were wrecked with heavy loss of life and

Lerwick's lifeboat men helped to widen the chink in the Iron Curtain as they risked their lives in saving "Russian" seamen.

A problem which was more difficult to solve was the large amount of debris discarded by those vessels during trans-shipping operations. This caused serious problems for the crews of local seine netters working in areas where those ships had been at anchor.

Shetland fishermen were concerned when Polish fishermen were given permission to establish a base for trans-shipment at Mitchell's yard at Lerwick. Their opposition to the project ensured that the lease was granted for one year only.

A regular pattern developed in the local herring fishery as boats started fishing in May, when the main outlet was the fish meal plant at Bressay, while in June the curers entered the market. In 1952 there were 13 curing firms based at Lerwick, while J. & M. Shearer was still operating at Cullivoe and Symbister. The firm gave up the Cullivoe operation after the 1954 season and that at Symbister in 1959.

The curers at Lerwick in 1952 were G. & J. Donaldson, Stuart Duthie & Co, W. Slater & Sons, J. Mair, P. W. Buchan, A. Wood & Sons, SCWS, A. Bremner & Co, G. J. Ross & Co, L. & J. Dunbar, J. & M. Shearer, A. Davidson & Co, and the Buckie Association. Others which commonly worked at Lerwick were Pommer & Thomson, Joe Slater and Sinclair and Buchan.

A seine netter working east of Shetland while vessels from the Soviet Union go about their own business on the horizon.

Photo – Bobby Tulloch

Kippering was still a major activity, with J. & M. Shearer and the HIB operating at Lerwick and the National Fish Curing Company and L. Williamson operating old fashioned kilns at Scalloway.

In the early part of the season, when the boats were working off the Ve Skerries or the Ramna Stacks, considerable quantities of herring were landed at Scalloway, most of it transferred by road to Lerwick, before the start of the main fishery on east side grounds.

When the main fishery failed the boats had to move farther afield. In the summer of 1953 most of the fleet moved to Wick. The following year the boats were even more widely spread, being based at Wick, Fraserburgh and Peterhead.

The numbers going to the autumn fishery at East Anglia also declined steadily. Twelve boats set out from Shetland in 1950 but one of them, the *Northern Light*, had to turn back. On her way south she had set her nets off the Humber and was on her way in to Grimsby to land a small catch of ten crans when a young Burra man, Matthew Cecil Cumming (26) fell overboard. He had lost his balance while hauling a rope as the crew made ready to land the catch. In spite of valiant attempts to save him by a crewman from the Grimsby trawler *Edinburgh Castle*, heading out to sea, he was swept away in the strong current and drowned. His body was recovered some days later.

The *Betty Leslie* was a regular and successful participant in the autumn fishery. In 1951 she had the highest earnings of any vessel in the Scottish fleet. In 1952 she was joined by the *John West*, *Mary Watt* and *Jessie Sinclair*. That was the *Mary Watt*'s last season under Shetland owners as she was sold to owners in Peterhead.

In 1953 the *Betty Leslie* was joined by the *John West*, *Jessie Sinclair* and *Dauntless*, after a dreadful season at Shetland when the herring were so scarce that the Herring Industry Board chartered the *Wave Sheaf* to spend a week searching for shoals around Shetland. In 1954 the *Betty Leslie* had only one companion from Shetland, the *Jessie Sinclair*, which was to steal the show that year by winning the Prunier Trophy for the top shot of the season – one of 272 crans taken on 12th of October.

The crew of the Burra boat *Jessie Sinclair* after landing a shot of 270 crans on 12th October, 1954, to take the Prunier Trophy for that year's top landing at the East Anglian herring fishing. Back row (from left): Willie Goodlad, Jeemie Christie, George Cogle, Bob Williamson (skipper); Sinclair Goodlad and Charles Christie. Front row (from left): John Williamson, Tammie Inkster, Willie Laurenson and Geordie Hunter (mate).

Photo – Robert Johnson collection

In 1955 there were no Shetland boats at East Anglia, but the *Betty Leslie*, no longer based in Shetland, had several Shetlanders among her crew. The *Jessie Sinclair* did not return to Lowestoft until 1958 when she was accompanied by the *Ocean Reaper*, whose skipper Geordie Hunter had been mate on the *Jessie Sinclair* when she won the trophy. A third Burra boat was the *Venture*. Results that year were very disappointing.

In 1957 a new price structure was established in the herring fishery whereby, for the first time since the war, herring were exposed for auction with minimum prices of 60/- a cran for curing, 74/- for kippering and 87/- for fresh fish outlets. Only 18 local boats took part in the fishery at Shetland.

That year for the first time herring fishermen were eligible for a subsidy from the Government, a payment for each day's fishing, which had been available for white fish boats for several years.

This payment led to an unprecedented strike of half catch men from Burra – those without shares in boats or nets. The dispute centred on the question of whether the subsidy should be paid into the vessel's gross earnings or shared among the crew.

The strike ended after a few days with an agreement to increase each crewmember's weekly "stoker" money – a few pounds paid weekly as subsistence money until the main settlement was made at the end of the season – with £1 a week coming off the subsidy.

White fish becomes more important

As the seine net fishery became more important, at the expense of the herring fishery, catches of haddock and whiting increased dramatically until in 1951 the value of this sector exceeded that of the herring fishery for the first time – a total of £144,000 compared with £93,000 earned by the herring fishery that year. The gap widened until in 1956 the value of white fish caught by Shetland boats exceeded £350,000, while the value of herring landed that year by local boats and several from parts in the north-east of Scotland was a mere £112,000.

Local markets found it even more difficult to cope with the huge landings of haddock and whiting and the practice of "tripping" to Aberdeen became still more important. This was a double loss to Shetland, since after landing their catches at Aberdeen market the boats took on ice, fuel and stores before returning to the fishing grounds.

In 1954 skipper John Leask and some of his crew decided that it would be far more convenient to set up homes in Aberdeen to enable them to spend their weekend break at home with their families.

Fortunately for Shetland this did not set a precedent. The other fishermen decided to stay in Shetland even though the time spent with their families was limited. Later it became the practice to leave one or two men at home at the end of each fishing trip before the vessel headed for Aberdeen.

Most crews tried to reach Aberdeen on a Saturday morning which gave their boat a good position at the head of the market on Monday morning when merchants, eager to get consignments on their way to customers as early as possible, paid the highest prices at the start of the sale. Another benefit from a Saturday arrival was the opportunity for a night on the town after a hard week at sea.

In order to catch enough fish to justify the added expense of tripping, the boats had to work almost round the clock for three or four days. They were generally working near Shetland and could call at Scalloway or Lerwick to complete the gutting, washing, boxing and icing of the catch.

If the weather forecast was bad they had no alternative but to land their catches for sale "on the pier" or ship the fish to Aberdeen by the steamer from Lerwick, and then start a new fishing trip.

This was a last resort and those running to Aberdeen had some horrendous experiences on the 200 mile journey in small boats, heavily loaded with between 150 and 250 boxes of fish on board, depending on the size of the vessel.

Approaching Aberdeen there was the added worry that the port might be closed due to a problem with the harbour entrance, which is often unsafe in an easterly gale as heavy seas surge up the navigation channel between the two breakwaters.

The Burra boat *Sunshine II* had an alarming experience as she entered the channel in March 1958. A huge wave caught her on the port quarter and hurled her towards the north breakwater, laying her almost on her beam ends. The next wave sent her out of control towards the south breakwater. At one point she was so far over that the deckhouse touched the sea. Fortunately she survived the ordeal.

The reward for all the dangers involved in tripping was the price to be obtained for their catch – usually far higher than that obtained in Shetland, even after taking into account the extra fuel consumed on the journey and the two days spent on the journey. Most marked was the higher price obtained for the small quantities of flatfish, cod, hake, etc caught in addition to the main species.

In the autumn of 1958 the Whalsay boat *La Morlaye* became the first Shetland vessel to break the £1000 barrier for a catch at Aberdeen. This record was broken a few days later when the *Serene* earned £1328 for 325 boxes.

There were hazards on the journey quite apart from the weather. In 1958 the old Fifie *Jeannie*, returning home to Whalsay after landing her catch at Aberdeen, was in collision with an Aberdeen trawler 11 miles off Peterhead. Although she had suffered extensive damage the crew kept the *Jeannie* afloat and brought her to Peterhead. Problems with the insurers led to a delay in repairs being carried out and Robert Shearer and his crew fished with other boats before they bought the Burra boat *Dauntless* and renamed her *Silver Chord*.

After being repaired, the *Jeannie* was sold by J. & M. Shearer to Herring By-Products Ltd to carry fish offal and surplus fish from Lerwick to the fish meal factory at Bressay. A few years later she was taken to Leiraness Voe in Bressay, where she was beached and eventually broken up.

Earlier in 1958 the inshore fishing vessel *Star Divine* was run down by the Aberdeen trawler *Ben Urie* while hauling lines south of Lerwick. A dense fog had come down and the trawler was unaware of the small boat. Skipper George Nicol and his three-man crew survived the incident. Two of them clambered onto the trawler while the other was rescued by the trawler's crew.

On the fishing grounds in winter the seine netters were often working near the limit of their capabilities. While most fishermen had frightening experiences none came closer to disaster than the crew of the Burra boat *Replenish*.

On 9th December, 1957, when heading back for Burra since the weather was too stormy for fishing, the *Replenish* was struck by two mountainous seas while in the area of the Ve Skerries. The first struck her aft, swinging her off course and leaving the starboard side exposed for the next blow. Most of the wooden deckhouse, the small boat carried at the stern and all moveable gear was swept away.

Skipper John L. Pottinger was half in the water when he managed to grab hold of the rail and pull himself onboard. Unknown to him five of the crew, whom he assumed were in their bunks in the cabin, had been standing in the

The Burra boat *Replenish* at Scalloway with the sturdy new deckhouse which replaced the one wrecked by the sea.

Photo – Robert Johnson

galley and all of them were now struggling in the sea. One of them managed to grab hold of a rope and haul himself onboard. The other four managed to get into the small boat, which was half full of water, and after a considerable time, using a piece of wood as a paddle, they managed to reach the *Replenish*.

The skipper's oldest son, John William Pottinger, had taken the first watch at the wheel after leaving Burra and he was sleeping in the cabin when the boat suddenly heeled over. As seawater poured down the hatch he was convinced that the boat was sinking.

The skipper's first task was to put the engine out of gear, to prevent the propeller from becoming fouled by the lengths of seine net rope which had been washed overboard and were trailing astern. With the help of the two men he began to hack away over 20 lengths of rope using a knife.

There remained the problem of recovering the men from the water-logged lifeboat. Somehow, almost miraculously, the boat drifted close to the *Replenish* and the occupants were hauled onboard. Then the *Replenish* headed for her moorings at Easter Dale, Burra. The men were examined by the doctor from Scalloway and found to be remarkably well in spite of their ordeal.

Next day the *Replenish* headed for Scalloway where she discharged 80 boxes of fish caught earlier in the week. After temporary repairs had been carried out she went south to Fraserburgh to have a new wheelhouse fitted – one made from steel.

The *Replenish* incident provided a clue to the cause of the disappearance of the Peterhead boat *Still Waters* two years earlier. From that time a steel wheelhouse became a standard fitting in new vessels built in Scotland. The incident also added weight to the campaign to have inflatable life-rafts made compulsory for fishing vessels.

Facilities onshore remained basic in most areas and several boats were damaged or wrecked as they dragged their anchors and drove ashore during a gale. Those that became a total loss included the small seiner *Water Lily* at Hamnavoe, the *Britannia* at Scalloway and the larger vessel *Verdant* at South Voe in Whalsay. She had been bought only a few months previously.

Piers were built in the 1950s at Out Skerries and Hamnavoe but they did nothing to improve shelter. Only at Lerwick was a considerable improvement made in the late 1950s when, in addition to improvements at Victoria Pier, an arm was constructed extending northwards from the end of the pier and a spur jetty was built near the south end of Alexandra Wharf. In June 1959 work began on a new covered fish marked for the landing and sale of white fish.

The situation at Whalsay deteriorated when the jetty owned by J. & M. Shearer was washed away during the storm of 4th February, 1953. This gale caused widespread havoc throughout the UK and is best remembered in Shetland for the loss of two men from Nesting, Harry and Harold Gear, who had gone out in a small boat to haul their haddock lines.

Those were difficult years for the inshore seine netters. Too small to "trip" to Aberdeen they were at the mercy of local markets which were now dominated by Fromac. While the firm provided the main outlet for fish landed in Shetland its involvement with Shetland was an unhappy one for local fishermen. The firm was competing with processors in Scotland and England who did not have such high transport costs and so had to get its raw material as cheaply as possible.

Agreements were made with fishermen to land their catches for a guaranteed quota, which varied from day to day, while over-quota fish would be bought by the company almost as a concession at prices as low as 9d (old pence) per stone.

Another problem faced by the company was that the fish landed by smaller boats was handled less carefully than the catches of bigger boats. The firm

Part of the Whalsay
fishing fleet at
anchor in South Voe.

Photo – Ian
Anderson

tried very hard to entice some of the larger vessels to land their catches locally instead of tripping. While some tested the local market from time to time, landing "on the pier" was still a last resort in most cases.

The crews of small boats had other problems to face. These vessels were usually under-powered and this led to a loss of fish through the meshes of the codend. To overcome this most crews used codends with a mesh opening smaller than the legal minimum of two inches along each side of the diamond mesh. Almost every month one or more skippers were fined in Lerwick Sheriff Court, after having their codends checked by the local fishery officer during his routine examinations.

Their income depended on landing as much fish as possible, given the low prices paid, and in trying to do so they were often taken to court for landing fish smaller than the legal minimum size of 11 inches for haddock and nine inches for whiting.

Fishery protection vessels kept a regular watch over inshore waters, arresting vessels over 50 feet long when caught fishing within the three-mile limit. They ignored the fact that fishing ability depended more on horse power than over all length and it was galling for crews of boats like the *Celerity* – old and under-powered but a few inches longer than 50 feet – to be penalised so often in this way. The skipper of the *Maid of the Mist* solved the problem for his vessel by taking a saw and cutting about three inches off the top of the boat's stern post.

Changes were made in the regulations from time to time. From 5th April, 1954, the minimum mesh size was increased to 70mm. In October 1958 a new by-law (No 57) removed the ban on fishing during darkness within the three mile limit. This came as a result of a petition by the skippers of 22 boats on 3rd May that year.

It is not surprising to find that marketing problems figured largely at meetings of Shetland Fishermen's Association throughout the 1950s and that skippers of white fish vessels generally held the post of chairman of the association.

The post was vacated by John Leask, when he moved to Aberdeen, and the association's secretary Jeemie Pottinger served as chairman until Jeemie Alex Watt of Scalloway, skipper of the *Pilot Us*, was appointed chairman in 1955. He was replaced in 1957 by Robbie Watt of Lerwick, skipper of the *Harvest Gold*, while in 1958 Geordie Hunter of Burra, skipper of the *Ocean Reaper*, held the post. In 1959 John James Fullerton of Scalloway was elected to the post. He had acquired the 48ft long *Bonnie Isle* from Whalsay and renamed her *Brighter Hope*. He was to serve as chairman until 1963.

A co-operative approach

In 1952 the Scottish Committee of the White Fish Authority looked at the problems faced by Shetland fishermen and recommended that a co-operative should be set up to market fish and to purchase fishing gear, stores, etc in bulk, thus reducing the cost to members.

This recommendation was adopted at a meeting of Shetland Fishermen's Association on 24th May, 1955. A committee was formed with Geordie Hunter as chairman. Before the end of that year Shetland Fish Ltd was in business with premises at Scalloway and later at Lerwick. It acted as fish salesmen, handling the accounts of member vessels, and tried to find markets for all the fish caught by its members.

In 1957 it started a new venture, following the example of Norwegian fishermen, catching dogfish which were abundant in waters around Shetland at that time. The dogfish, after being landed at Scalloway and Lerwick, were skinned and dispatched to a market in England. A young Norwegian Arve Hovden, who had married a Shetland girl, Leila Ramsay, was employed as adviser to teach Shetland fishermen how to rig the lines used in this fishery and provide the suitable equipment on deck.

Surprisingly the Shetland product could not compete as regards price and quality with imports from Norway.

Nevertheless this fishery continued for several years, providing an important source of income for several crews and providing seasonal employment for a number of men at Lerwick and Scalloway.

Shetland Fish Ltd received very little support locally, the White Fish Authority having put up almost 90 per cent of the capital required. A bigger problem was that it did not have the support of the bigger vessels in the local fleet. With only two exceptions the big boats remained loyal to LHD Ltd.

The difficulties faced by Shetland Fish Ltd added to the mood of pessimism which pervaded Shetland at that time. It was therefore surprising that a group of businessmen should consider this an opportune time to start a fish processing venture at Scalloway.

The inspiration for the project came from Captain Adam Tait, well known to many Shetlanders at that time as senior lecturer in navigation and seamanship on the training ship *Dolphin* attached to Leith Nautical College. During frequent holidays in Scalloway he was concerned at the steady downturn in the economic life of the village and he persuaded a group of friends to join him in a fish processing project.

An approach was made to Zetland County Council for support but the council's convener drew the group's attention to the vast amounts of fish which were by-passing Shetland and being landed by local boats at Aberdeen. He added that in his opinion the fishing was "finished" as far as Shetland was concerned.

When the project was evaluated it was found that it would require an investment of £60,000 – an enormous sum in those days. An approach was made to the White Fish Authority for grant assistance; but this was declined since the Authority had come to the conclusion that Aberdeen should be the main centre for all fishing activity in the North of Scotland. Moreover the White Fish Authority was still smarting from its unhappy experience with Shetland Fish Ltd.

Vital support for the project at Scalloway came from Andrew Anderson, still involved with the White Fish Authority in an advisory capacity. In a 20 minute speech at a meeting in Edinburgh he pointed out that Shetland was at the centre of the best fishing grounds in the North Sea and must be the best location for a fish processing plant.

The outcome of his speech was that the Authority decided to give a grant of £30,000 towards the project. Some local people were encouraged to take shares in the venture and the balance was taken equally among the directors of the company.

Alex S. Fraser decided to leave his job as agent for the "North of Scotland" shipping company to serve as managing director. The other directors were Captain Tait; Alex Munro, a general merchant in Edinburgh; James Tait, a fish merchant in Leith; and Gerald B. Silver, a chartered accountant in Glasgow. Mr Thomas Fraser, a fully qualified marine engineer, gave up his seafaring career to become manager.

The company's name was chosen by Adam Tait. During a camping holiday in his caravanette the trade name on the sleeping bag – Icelandic – caught his attention. The factory was concerned with ice and Scalloway was on the Atlantic side of Shetland – so why not Iceatlantic?

The factory started production in 1959, producing frozen fillets of white fish while the offal was converted into high grade protein-rich fish meal suitable for animal food. It had a hard struggle in its early years but was to provide the example required for the development of Shetland's fish processing industry under local control.

CHAPTER THREE

From famine to feast in the 1960s

Since the end of the war the fishing grounds around Shetland had provided a good living for an expanding fleet of seine netters from our own islands and the east coast of Scotland. Indeed boats from Buckie regarded the Burra Haaf as their summer fishing ground, working beside those from Burra and Scalloway, and joining them at Blacksness pier to clear up the last shot of the day.

It was assumed that a gradual expansion of the white fish sector could continue indefinitely – until events in the autumn of 1958 sent shock waves throughout the industry, as a scarcity of fish affected the fleet all round the islands.

The catch of 1958 was still impressive with 191,000 cwts caught by Shetland boats, of which 112,000 cwts were landed at Shetland ports. In 1959 the total catch was reduced to 142,000 cwts, of which 89,000 were landed at Shetland, and in 1960 only 86,000 cwts of which 53,000 cwts were landed locally. Landings were to remain at this low level for another two years.

The drop in landings was alleviated to a minor extent by higher quayside prices as Macfisheries had to compete for supplies. It was also faced with the threat of competition from Iceatlantic – still an unknown force in Shetland.

The plant at Scalloway was ready in May 1960. It could not have started at a worse time since supplies of fish were erratic and the prices higher that

Blacksness pier with Iceatlantic in the early 1960s.

Photo – C. J. Williamson

expected. In 1960 for the first time the average price paid at local markets for white fish exceeded £2 per cwt. Another two merchants were involved – Suttons and John Laurie, who had bought Dunbar's station at Lerwick as his base.

The scarcity of fish was an important factor in the ultimate failure of Shetland Fish Ltd. The directors claimed that the co-operative had made a profit in its first year; but then came a slump in fish landings, leading to a reduction in the commission earned on fish sent to market, with the result that its overheads could not be covered.

Shetland Fish Ltd was wound up in September 1961 with liabilities of around £17,000. Some skippers in Scalloway, who had left the LHD agency to support the co-op were unwilling to admit publicly their failure, by going "cap in hand" back to LHD Ltd, approached Alex S. Fraser and he agreed to act as their salesman. One or two boats in Lerwick which had been in membership of the co-operative also operated under the agency of ASF.

Shetland Fish's biggest achievement was to develop the fishery for dogfish, which gave the smaller boats – the most vulnerable in the fleet – an alternative to seine netting. In 1957 it had paid out £15,300 for 17,300 cwts of dogfish. In 1960 this activity was worth £7,700, while those employed ashore in skinning the fish earned £2000 in part-time employment.

These activities continued after the demise of Shetland Fish Ltd as Alex Fraser took over the processing operation at Scalloway and Harry Gray obtained the lease of Number One station at Lerwick, previously let to the co-operative.

The scarcity of fish hit the small boats hard during the winter months. A few boats at Scalloway, working haddock lines, made good catches on hard bottom where the seine netters could not operate. It was claimed that the *Fruitful* (skipper Ernie Duncan) had set a record for a line fishing boat by making a gross earning of £369 in the week ending 15th January, 1959.

Another two boats joined the Whalsay fleet in 1959 – the 66ft long *Zephyr* built by J. & G. Forbes of Sandhaven for skipper Lowrie Irvine and partners, and the *Fruitful Bough* (skipper Willie Irvine) as a replacement for the *Verdant*, which had been wrecked while lying at her moorings. The star of this period, however, was the *Dauntless II* built for skipper Alex John Henry and partners of Hamnavoe. With an overall length of 75 feet she was the biggest vessel in Shetland at that time.

The next two years saw a decline in the islands' white fish fleet with several boats being sold outwith Shetland. They included the Scalloway boats *Silver Cloud* and *Pathfinder*; the Burra boats *Still Waters* and *Southern Cross*; the Whalsay boat *Xmas Rose*; the Lerwick boats *Harvest Hope* and *Our Queen* (formerly of Whalsay); and the *Budding Rose* and *Endeavour*, the two boats which had kept alive the tradition of fishing at Whiteness.

In 1961 the engine was taken from the old *Golden Lily* (built in 1935) and installed in the *Cornucopia*, now owned by skipper Alex Goodlad and partners. Soon afterwards Mr Goodlad moved to Aberdeen. Another change of ownership affected the *Betty Leslie*, still fondly remembered in Shetland. She was sold to a Fleetwood company and renamed *Boston Mosquito*. Years later she was to gain notoriety when, as the *April Diamond*, she was arrested for carrying illegal immigrants to Britain.

Five more boats were sold in 1963 – the *Winner*, *Wave Sheaf*, *Liberty*, *Fair Dawn* and *Village Maid*. During those years when so many boats left the Shetland fleet there were only two additions – the 41ft long *Jan el Mar*, bought from Wick by owners in Burra and renamed *Girl Ann*, and the *Rosetta*. They were bought mainly for lobster fishing. By this time the local fleet had shrunk to only 48 boats over 40ft long.

Most of these changes were due to "natural causes" although the poor returns may have been a contributing factor. It says much for the fishermen of that period that most of them stood by the industry.

A tragedy at the end of 1961 left a deep impression on the islands when two young Lerwick men were lost. John Wiseman (35) and his brother Albert (33) had acquired the inshore fishing vessel *Replenish* at Macduff. On their way north they stopped at Wick, leaving there on Saturday 30th December. They were never seen again. It is assumed that the boat was overwhelmed by heavy seas off Orkney.

Success of lobster fishing

A bright spot in this period of gloom was the rise of the fishery for lobsters. This had expanded steadily during the 1950s, usually as a part-time occupation, ancillary to crofting or some other job. It was encouraged in the early years by a local co-operative the Crofters Supply Agency, which operated the small fishing boat *Ord* for demonstration purposes.

The traditional Shetland model boat fitted with 1½ hp or 4hp Stuart Turner engine was considered adequate for working 50 or 60 creels set individually. Each day's catch was added to floating storage boxes anchored in a sheltered location, and after a week or so the catch was packed in a wooden tea chest, with wet sawdust as filling, and dispatched to merchants in Billingsgate or elsewhere.

The lobster was already being fished heavily in several parts of Scotland and the danger of overfishing was apparent to many people, including Sir Basil Neven-Spence as MP for Orkney and Shetland. On 1st May, 1951, a new order based on his recommendation came into force, stipulating that the minimum length of a lobster offered for sale should be increased from 8 inches to 9 inches, as measured along the main shell, and prohibiting the landing of lobsters carrying spawn. That year 29,000 lobsters were landed at Shetland valued at around £7,000. Sir Basil was no longer an MP, having been ousted from the seat by Jo Grimond in the 1950 election.

Lobster fishing was a dangerous occupation, especially during the winter. Shetland's climate is notoriously fickle and a fisherman, having set his creels on the sheltered side of an island or voe, could find that the wind had changed direction overnight and he had to haul his creels on a lee shore.

Several men lost their lives in this fishery – four in 1961 alone. They included two young men from Scalloway, Bruce Leask and Walter Jamieson,

The *Homeland* with a load of lobster creels. Her skipper at this time was Geordie Leslie.

Photo – James R. Sinclair

whose boat foundered as it was rounding the Bard of Bressay on its way to Lerwick.

A major problem for lobster fishermen was the lack of outlets for their catch in Shetland. This was solved in 1961 when a Scalloway man James Watt, the manager of the Co-op shop in the village, proved that lobsters could be kept alive out of the sea for long periods, in tanks provided with circulating sea water, where they could be held until market prices were at their highest.

Mr Watt decided to make this his full-time occupation and set up the company Scalloway Shellfish Ltd, with storage tanks at Port Arthur holding up to 10,000 pounds of lobsters. He found a lucrative market in Britanny and sent consignments regularly by air from Sumburgh. One weekend, when his lobster ponds were full, he was forced to use the children's paddling pool beside Scalloway's Main Street as additional storage.

Soon after this a Lerwick businessman John Laurie had storage ponds built at Lerwick as part of his expansion into the shellfish trade.

As the scarcity of white fish continued throughout 1961, many of the biggest seine netters switched over to lobster fishing and the catch soared to unprecedented levels. In 1956 the total value of shellfish landed at Shetland was a mere £10,000 but by 1961 this had soared to £87,500 and a year later to £114,000 for 5390 cwts – mainly lobsters.

It was a strange experience for the crews of the largest white fish vessels to be working so close to the shore. One of them, the old *Northern Light*, was lost in April 1961 when she struck a rock and sank off the Ness of Hillswick, fortunately without loss of life. Other boats found safer working conditions – and good catches – around Foula.

It was obvious to many people that the lobster stock was being fished far beyond its maximum sustainable yield and could not withstand for long such an intensive fishery. It was fortunate that the white fish stocks began to recover in 1963, thus easing the pressure on the lobster fishery.

With the threat from the big boats removed, the regular lobster fishermen embarked on a period of development, with better equipped boats, designed to handle more creels more efficiently. The first boats built under the White Fish Authority's new grant and loan scheme in 1959 were the *Utopian* for Raffie Angus Cumming, built by Walter Duncan of Hamnavoe, and the *Robina*, built by Jesse Goudie of Scalloway for Gibby Johnson of Vidlin. Mr Johnson was later to build his own lobster storage ponds and was soon a major buyer of shellfish in the North Mainland.

The expansion of the lobster fishery led to an expansion of boat building in Shetland. Walter Duncan's boatshed at Hamnavoe was as busy as at any time in its long history. Jesse Goudie and Robert Walterson at Scalloway, James Smith at Lerwick and A. Sandison and Sons of Baltasound were all kept busy during the next few years, while a new boat building firm, Shetland Marine, was started at Lerwick by J. B. A. Sutherland.

The end of whaling in the Antarctic made an impact on the lobster fishing at Shetland. Christian Salvesen & Company, recognising the contribution made to the firm by men from

The purpose-built lobster boat *Utopian* anchors for the night at Ham, Foula, in 1962. The crew are Tom Thomson from Quarff (left) and skipper Raffie Angus Cumming from Burra.

Photo –Duncan Cumming

Shetland, some of whom regarded the annual voyage to South Georgia as their main source of employment, set up the Salvesen Trust in 1964, with funds of £33,000. Its aim was to provide grants to allow ex-whalers to acquire small fishing boats. The first to do so were Michael Jamieson and Andy Smith from Aith, who acquired the 30ft long *Sheena* from Orkney.

White fish stocks recover

The lowest point in the depression caused by the decline of white fish stocks came in 1962, when only 58,100 cwts were landed at Shetland worth £125,000, while landings by Shetland boats at Aberdeen amounted to 51,000 cwts worth £147,000. A significant recovery took place the following year, when landings at Shetland increased to 80,000 cwts valued at £170,000, while Shetland boats tripping to Aberdeen landed 132,000 cwts valued at £323,000.

In November 1963 the Burra boat *Sceptre* established a new record for a Shetland boat landing her catch at Aberdeen – a total of £1578 for 298 cwts. This was to stand until May the following year when the Whalsay boat *La Morlaye* again held the record with a gross of £1901 for 270 cwts.

With better returns from the white fish and a good summer for those boats changing over to herring fishing there was less need for the big boats to switch over to lobster fishing that winter. There was also less incentive to do so since it was clear that the lobster stocks had taken a hammering during the previous two winters. In 1963 the lobster catch was well down at 1807 cwt worth £60,000, while the following year it dropped further to 1388 cwts worth £53,000.

The slump in white fish stocks was studied in detail by fisheries scientists, who pointed out that it was due to a serious decline in the haddock stock, while catches of whiting remained remarkably steady.

Generally speaking the fishable stock of haddock contains fish of only four or five year classes. While the failure of a single year class, due to poor spawning conditions, has little impact on the stocks and the fishery, a succession of poor year classes has a disastrous effect. This was the situation in 1961, following several years when spawning conditions had been poor.

In 1961 it seemed to many fishermen that there was hardly a haddock left in the sea. Then a remarkable occurrence took place in 1962 when that year produced an exceptionally strong brood of haddock. It was due to a combination of factors, the eggs hatching when conditions were ideal, with the correct temperature, salinity and availability of food.

By the end of 1963 fishermen were reporting large quantities of small haddock passing through the meshes of the codends while herring fishermen were noticing small haddock on the surface.

In 1964 the young haddock were between 10 and 11 inches long and fishermen found it frustrating to have to discard large quantities of these fish because they were a fraction of an inch under the marketable size.

Having survived the worst of the recession, Macfisheries took everyone by surprise when it suspended operations early in November 1962. The manager made it clear that the firm might resume operations if a sufficient number of skippers were prepared to sign a contract guaranteeing supplies.

The threat had the desired effect and in February 1963 the firm was back in business with 60 workers re-engaged. The firm announced that 35 skippers had agreed to land their catches locally at a fixed price of 5/3d per stone for haddock, 4/6d per stone for large whiting and 2/9d for seed whiting, the catch to be allocated among the various buyers according to their share of the overall capacity. Small quantities of fish would be auctioned for the retail trade – the fish shops in Lerwick and the travelling vans which now covered most of Shetland. By this time most of the shipping buyers had given up this activity because of high freight charges and better demand at home.

The scheme worked well throughout 1963 with more than one thousand · tonnes of haddock and whiting being handled by Macfisheries and Iceatlantic. In January 1964, at a meeting of the association, fishermen announced their intention to end this agreement and return to the auction system with the safeguard of new minimum prices.

This was the last straw for Macfisheries, who refused to accept the minimum prices as proposed and announced its decision to stop the processing of white fish in Shetland later that year.

This announcement came as a bombshell to Lerwick Town Council, who feared that it would lead to large scale unemployment in the town. Talks between the two parties in a bid to resolve the crisis came to nothing. Councillors claimed that Macfisheries was not really interested in Shetland, regarding its operation at Fraserburgh as far more important.

The despondency that followed the withdrawal of Macfisheries from Lerwick was followed by rising optimism, as new processing firms filled the gap and existing firms expanded their operation, helped greatly by the attitude of the fishermen, who reintroduced a fish allocation system with the safeguard of minimum prices.

At Scalloway Iceatlantic Seafoods extended its premises, expanded its white fish operation and installed Torry kilns for kippering herring. This compensated to some extent for a loss sustained in the village in March 1963 when the National Fishcuring Company's kiln at Midshore was destroyed by fire.

In 1964 a second white fish processing plant was established at Scalloway when Thomas Fraser, formerly manager of Iceatlantic, started his own business in conjunction with his father Alex Fraser, the former managing director of Iceatlantic, as TTF (Fish Processing) Ltd.

The village had benefited greatly from the new breakwater at Blacksness which had been completed in 1961. This was followed by a covered fish market, which was less successful since it was built on the old quay, where there was insufficient depth of water to allow the newer, bigger boats to discharge their catches there. Moreover it was far too small for the increasing catches of white fish, which were landed wherever a berth was free, either on the south side of the old quay or along the new extension.

A rising star at Lerwick was John (Jock) Laurie who had started in a small way as a fish merchant and in 1962 started to process shellfish including crab. As J. & W. Laurie the firm was soon to acquire Scalloway Shellfish Ltd, when that firm was faced with severe financial problems. In October 1963 Mr Laurie's firm was reorganised as Shetland Seafoods with a 50 per cent holding by Youngs Seafoods. It then announced plans for new premises adjacent to the original building at Dunbar's station.

In January 1965 Shetland Seafoods began to process white fish in the Herring Industry Board's factory at Lerwick, having signed an agreement with the Board similar to the contract held previously by Macfisheries.

Another new firm at Lerwick was Blair & Smith who had a new factory built in April 1968 and became one of the "big four" in the white fish processing sector, as well as handling a considerable quantity of herring.

As the catch of white fish increased and the range of species widened, processing plants were established throughout the northern half of Shetland in the late 1960s and early 1970s. At Scalloway the long established firm of L. Williamson converted its fish shed and smokehouse into a modern processing plant, commenced a fish processing plant at Lerwick and had a fish meal plant as part of the firm's operation at Wethersta near Brae. In 1971 the firm opened a branch at Kirkwall, obtaining supplies of white fish from the Orkney fishing fleet.

Gibby Johnson of Vidlin invested heavily in the processing industry with a plant at Graven known as Sullom Voe Shellfish. Partners in the business were Robert van Smirren, who had a crab cannery at Boston, Linc., and local man Arthur Manson. Mr Johnson also set up a white fish and shellfish processing plant at Skerries and was a major shareholder in a similar plant at Ronas Voe.

A small white fish processing operation was started in a redundant school building at Brough, Whalsay in 1970 by John Tait. When its viability was proved the company was reorganised with investment by around 20 local fishermen and a large new plant was built near the island's fishing harbour. A large breakwater had been built for Shetland Islands Council in the South Voe in 1964 putting an end to the controversy that had raged for years over the best site for a harbour at Whalsay. Fish processing started at Easterdale, Burra, in 1972 with investment by the Henry Brothers and Gibby Johnson

The island of Yell, long affected by unemployment, received two processing plants – one a shellfish operation run by Shetland-Norse, the other a white fish processing unit built by Shetland Seafoods and later acquired by Gibby Johnson. Mr Johnson had also turned his attention to Lerwick, being the main shareholder in the Arlanda factory at Gremista.

From a labour force of 200 in 1965 the numbers employed in fish processing in Shetland rose to just over 600 in 1970, including 120 employed only during the herring season. The value of fish products from Shetland's processing units in 1970 exceeded £2.5 million.

The search for "new" species

One of the most important developments of this period was the local outlets for crabs. Caught as a by-catch in lobster creels, a large proportion of the catch was simply thrown back into the sea. A few fishermen had sent consignments of crab to southern markets as early as the 1940s but most did not consider it worth while to do so. In 1962 only 861 cwt of crab had been landed at Shetland but in 1963 the catch increased to 4642 cwts with a value of £9284.

By the end of 1963 there were ten boats landing crabs at West Burrafirth using a small and very inadequate stone pier, and already Shetland Fishermen's Association was preparing its case for improvements in that area.

The Scalloway boat *Brighter Hope* seen here equipped for catching dogfish with a line chute at the stern.

Photo – James R. Sinclair

A man who played a major role in the search for "new" species to exploit was John James Fullerton, skipper of the 48ft long *Brighter Hope*. In 1966, while on holiday in the Moray Firth area, he went to sea on a boat fishing for sprats and noted that the marks seen on its echosounder were identical to those he had seen in his own vessel while fishing in St Magnus Bay.

Returning home he found a crew willing to take part in a pair trawling experiment, starting in November that year, and the results were so good that by the following February about a dozen boats were fishing for sprats in voes along the west side of Shetland; and they landed almost 30,000 cwts valued at over £10,000. Unfortunately the only outlet was the fish meal plant at Bressay.

The results were less rewarding the following season and thereafter insignificant. Those taking part in the fishery came to the conclusion that the stock had either been fished out or that sprats were not regular visitors to the area.

Scalloway fishermen Bobby Peterson, Jeemie Alex Watt and skipper John James Fullerton.

In 1968, on a visit to the west coast of Scotland, Mr Fullerton was impressed by the scale of the scallop fishery which had developed there. Realising that scallops were to be found around Shetland, being hauled up in the seine net and found clinging to haddock lines, he had the *Brighter Hope* fitted with a trawl winch and scallop dredges.

His two week experiment in November 1969 started with little success on the west side of Shetland. Moving to the east side results were less than promising, until the last day of the experiment, when the *Brighter Hope* was fishing along the west side of Yell Sound and encountered prolific beds of scallops off the Point of Fethaland.

Before starting his experiment Mr Fullerton had contacted Gibby Johnson, who negotiated a market for scallop meat and was ready to process the catch in his factory at Graven. Within a few weeks the *Brighter Hope* was joined by other vessels of this size and the fishery made rapid progress, becoming the mainstay of a sizeable part of the inshore fleet and providing a lasting alternative to seine netting whenever that fishery became unproductive.

The growing importance of the shellfish industry led to the establishment of a shellfish committee as part of the Shetland Fishermen's Association.

The fleet increases

With an improvement in the catch of white fish confidence returned to the industry, with new boats joining the fleet every year. In 1964 additions to the Whalsay fleet were the *Zenith* (skipper Arthur Polson) built at John Noble's yard at Fraserburgh and the *Amethyst* built for David Anderson.

In March 1965 there was a special welcome at Mid Yell for the *Concord*, built for skipper Ronnie Aitken and partners – the first new boat for Yell since the sailboat *Welcome Home* arrived in 1901. In May that year the 75ft long *Good Tidings* was bought by skipper Josie Simpson and partners. She was the first boat brought to Whalsay which did not require moorings, since she was able to take advantage of the new breakwater.

Additions to the Burra fleet at this time were the *Unison* (skipper Jeemsie Ward), *Radiant Star* (Bert Laurenson) and the *Gratitude*, a lovely new vessel built for John David Henry and partners.

1966 was a record year for new arrivals, the largest being the 70ft long

Evening Star, built for skipper Davie Smith and partners of Scalloway – a smart looking vessel with light blue hull and black bulwarks and a whaleback for'ard to provide more shelter for men working on deck. Another new boat for Yell was the smart little *Winsome* operating out of Cullivoe.

A number of good second hand boats arrived that year. The *Ros Donn* was bought by Andrew Spence and partners of Cullivoe, to replace the *St Vincent*

Sandy Anderson considers the work ahead for the crew in gutting a deck-full of fish on the Whalsay seine netter *Zenith*.

Photo – David Williamson

The Burra boat *Unison* (skipper Jeemsie Ward) takes onboard another lift from a full codend.

which was sold to Jeemie Watt and partners of Lerwick. The *Golden Grain*, which had been fishing off Macduff under skipper Bob Hay, became based at Burravoe in Yell.

Additions to the inshore fleet at Lerwick were the *Day Dawn* (skipper Taity Watt) and *Fertile* (skipper Peter Goodlad). The *Undaunted* was acquired by skipper Lowrie Bruce and partners of Burra while the *Spray* replaced the old *Sunbeam*, operated by skipper John Robert Watt of Scalloway. Another arrival at Scalloway the following year with the *Evangeline* (skipper Thomas Watt). By this time Shetland's fishing fleet had increased to 58 vessels over 40ft long.

In March 1968 the *Korona* was brought to Whalsay by skipper Peter Jamieson and partners. Designed for both seine netting and drift netting she was the last dual purpose vessel of this type to be built for Shetland. Later that year two second hand boats arrived for Scalloway owners – the *White Heather* for skipper Jeemie Robb and the *Milky Way* for skipper Magnus Sinclair and his son James. An addition to the seine net fleet at Whalsay was the *Heather Belle* for skipper Davie Hutchison and partners.

An interesting development in Yell was the arrival of the *Compass Rose* for a crew from Burravoe, the first to be built for Shetland owners under the Highlands & Islands Development Board's (HIDB) scheme to encourage fishing in areas where it was in danger of dying out.

The *Compass Rose* was built as a stern trawler, marking a break from the traditional pattern of seine net fishing which had dominated Shetland's fishing industry since the early 1940s. It is significant that in 1969 trawl landings figured in Shetland's fishery statistics for the first time, with a catch of 14,600 cwts valued at £33,000.

The benefit from the 1962 brood of haddock reached its peak in 1965, when 262,484 cwts of white fish were landed at Shetland worth £411,000 and landings at Aberdeen by Shetland boats were 40,000 cwts valued at £90,000. Local processors could not cope with such high landings and a further 55,000 cwts by-passed local markets, going direct to the fish meal factory at Bressay.

There were many occasions when local factories were so full of fish that

The stern trawler *Compass Rose* looking fresh after a refit at Scalloway.

Photo – Robert Johnson

crews were requested to fish on alternate days, usually for a limited quota. During those years local factories were working all out to make the most of the unexpected bonanza. Iceatlantic, the biggest of them, could process one thousand boxes a day, working three shifts. The firm had been restructured with heavy investment by the HIDB and the local council.

It was a case of mass production, the bulk of the catch being filleted and frozen into laminated block, a product which unfortunately attracted the lowest price when sold for secondary processing.

When marketing within the UK became difficult, the Scalloway firm TTF and shipping agent A. S. Fraser realised that there was an almost unlimited demand for laminated block in the USA and arranged for refrigerated cargo vessels to call regularly at Scalloway, on passage from Denmark to New England. The first to do so was the Icelandic vessel *Hofsjokull*, which berthed at Scalloway in April 1967 and loaded a consignment of 130 tons of frozen fish bound for Boston.

This was the start of a regular service between Scalloway and Gloucester and before long several plants in Shetland were using this service, the peak year being 1971 when 4500 tonnes were shipped from Scalloway valued at £1.5 million. By this time a large cold store had been built at Blacksness to accommodate consignments of frozen fish awaiting shipment to the USA.

Longer than the breakwater, the refrigerated cargo vessel *Echo* loads a cargo of frozen fish at Scalloway.

Photo – C. J. Williamson

The huge amounts of fish being landed at Scalloway forced a local sheep farmer Jim Smith to consider how gutting could be speeded up by mechanical means. At that time crews were still gutting the previous day's catch at 2 am or 3 am, then snatching a few hours sleep before heading back for the fishing grounds.

In 1966 Mr Smith patented a mechanical fish gutting machine which was manufactured in Aberdeen and installed in several British trawlers and seine netters. The inshore boat *Nil Desperandum* (skipper Jeemie Wiseman) was the first Shetland boat to have one installed. In 1971 Mr Smith developed and patented a fish selector to be used in conjunction with his gutting machine. For his services to the industry he was awarded the MBE.

After 1965 the white fish catch dropped to more normal levels as the haddock spawned in 1962 were fished out or fell victim to other predators. Then, as if one miracle wasn't enough, another occurred in 1967 when a haddock year class even stronger than that of 1962 appeared. This gave rise to the fantastic catch of 1971 when 417,800 cwts of white fish were caught by Shetland vessels worth £1,354,600.

In the meantime still more boats had joined the local fleet. In 1969 the stern trawler *Sapphire* was built for skipper A. M. Thomson and partners of Unst, the *Dewy Rose* (skipper Jeemie Gifford Leask) and *Silver Chord* (Willie Williamson) joined the Whalsay fleet and Jimmy Fullerton and partners of Hamnavoe bought the pocket trawler *Donvale*.

There were more changes at Whalsay in 1970 when Willie Simpson and partners bought the trawler *Ardsheean* to replace the *Brighter Morn*, which had been sold to John Peter Duncan and partners of Ollaberry, and Norman Poleson and partners bought the seine netter *Flourish*. An addition at Scalloway was the 70ft long *Sunbeam* for Magnus Sinclair and partners while the *Bairns Pride* came to Hamnavoe for Jess Inkster.

During 1970 a number of smaller boats, suitable for trawling and catching shellfish, were built for local fishermen. A. Sandison & Sons of Baltasound built the *Alert* for Jim Scott of Skeld and the *Ellida* for Unst man John Cluness, under the HIDB's scheme, and the *Lizanne* for A. H. Smith of Unst.

The Lerwick yard of J. B. A. Sutherland produced, among others, the *Tranquility* for Ronald Robertson of East Yell and the *Vestra* for William Hunter of Unst, while the *Shalimar* was built at Stromness for Campbell Gray of Mid Yell.

A number of boats left Shetland at this period, including the *Golden Acres* of Whalsay, the *Golden Harvest* and *Press On* of Burra, the *Halcyon* and *Golden Grain* from Yell and the Scalloway boats *Responsive* and *Brighter Hope*. The *Brighter Hope* was sold to Campbeltown, being replaced by a larger Norwegian vessel which was renamed *Brighter Hope II*.

A feature of the 1960s was the increasing use of electronic equipment, both in navigation and fish finding. In 1958 a Decca Navigator chain was provided for the North of Scotland with its master station in Orkney and slave stations at the Butt of Lewis, Peterhead and the Staney Hill outside Lerwick.

A peaceful scene at Cullivoe with the *Reliance* (built at Macduff in 1930) and *Tranquility* (built at Lerwick in 1969) lying at anchor.

Photo – Andrew Anderson

Shetland fishermen were now able to pin-point their positions with amazing accuracy and the inherited knowledge of meids was replaced quite quickly by Decca readings in a notebook, as practically every white fish vessel had Decca Navigator equipment installed.

Decca Navigator proved to be of special benefit to seine netters while working in foggy conditions it had often proved difficult to locate the dhan when completing the fishing triangle. With Decca Navigator in the wheelhouse it was a simple matter to record the position where the dhan was dropped and where it would be found again – allowing for movement by wind and tide.

As important was the introduction of radar sets for fishing vessels which removed to a great extent the anxiety felt when approaching a poorly lit coastline in a murky winter's night. It is understood that the Whalsay boat *Silver Chord* was the first to have radar installed – a Kelvin Hughes type 17.

In 1966 the Scalloway firm H. Williamson & Sons set up a subsidiary company Sonic Services (Marine) Ltd and acquired the agency for Decca radar and autopilots and Simrad echosounders and sonars. The staff of the Decca station at Lerwick were responsible for servicing Decca equipment for a further two years until that too became the responsibility of the Scalloway firm.

The Association in the 1960s

John James Fullerton, skipper of the Scalloway boat *Brighter Hope*, served as chairman of Shetland Fishermen's Association from 1959 to 1963 when he was succeeded by Geordie Hunter, skipper of the Burra boat *Ocean Reaper*, back for a second term. He served for a year when he was succeeded by Ronnie Aitken of Yell, skipper of the *Concord*. He served from 1964 to 1966 when he was replaced by Davie Anderson from Whalsay, skipper of the *Amethyst*. His successor another Whalsay man Josie Simpson, skipper of the *Good Tidings,* served as chairman from 1969 to 1971.

A problem discussed at a special general meeting on 17th December, 1960, was the reduction in money available for disbursement under a benevolent fund administered by the association – a drop of over £250 compared with the previous year. It was agreed that drastic economies would have to be made and that former fishermen able to perform light work such as machine knitting, net mending of lobster fishing near the shore should not be eligible for assistance.

The secretary later reported that this decision had led to such antagonism that he wished to disassociate himself from the work of the fund. It was then agreed to disburse the remainder of the fund – around a thousand pounds – to fishermen who were in obvious need. The first beneficiaries in April 1961 were the crew of the *Northern Light* which had sunk in St Magnus Bay. Skipper James Watt received £70 and his two deckhands £15 each.

As the association's secretary Jeemie Pottinger approached the age of 65 he was invited to remain as secretary and continue in an honorary capacity on half salary of £100 per annum. On 12th January, 1963, it was agreed to make a gift of £20 in appreciation of his services. In February 1965 it was discovered that Mr Pottinger had been using his own typewriter for association work since being appointed to the post in May 1939. This machine had broken and was found to be past repair so the meeting agreed that he should be given "a good second-hand machine" to compensate "for the use he had made of his own machine over the years."

Mr Pottinger's honorary position did not last long. His work load increased steadily over the next few years and on 18th December, 1965, it was agreed that his fee should be increased to £200 per annum. The amount of work continued to increase and on 4th October, 1969, it was raised to £350, the association paying his income tax.

Throughout this period marketing arrangements occupied much of the time at each meeting of the association. This became most acute from 1964 onwards when catches increased to such an extent that local outlets found it difficult to cope with supplies and large quantities of fish were sent to Bressay for conversion to fish meal at prices as low as 9d per stone.

The situation was most difficult in summer when some of the plants were engaged on herring processing and the restrictions were imposed to limit the amount of fish that could be landed. Boats might be allowed to fish only on alternate days or to land a limited number of boxes depending on the size of the crew. While the agreements signed by the majority of skippers were designed to limit the amount of fish being landed in Aberdeen, there was never any reduction and this practice continued throughout the 1960s while in times of plenty "tripping" was a useful method of avoiding gluts of fish.

The processors insisted that fish should be iced at sea, a stipulation which the smaller boats found it difficult to comply with. In practice most of these boats boxed and iced their catches while they were lying at the pier.

There were frequent complaints about the weights estimated by the merchant who had bought them. It was assumed that a box designed to hold six stone of fish would hold five stone when ice was put at the bottom and above the fish. There were times when the merchant's returns showed less than this. It was to overcome this problem that in September 1966 the association agreed that two men should be appointed to check weights whenever a dispute arose – in which case one box in every six would be weighed. Scales were provided for this purpose by LHD Ltd.

From 14 applicants a short list of six was selected and after a secret ballot James Christie was appointed to the job at Lerwick and John Robert Tait at Scalloway. It was agreed that a special levy of 1½d per pound of a boat's earnings would meet this expense. A separate account was inaugurated known as the SFA weights account. Mr Tait died in 1969 and he was replaced at Scalloway by Walter Jamieson.

Early in 1962 a problem arose when a lady was appointed manager of the employment exchange in Lerwick. Fishermen who had left port only to turn back because of bad weather found that she had turned down their application for unemployment benefit for that day.

It emerged that the new manager was adhering rigidly to the clause which stipulated that fishermen could not claim benefit when a fishing trip was unsuccessful – for example because of engine problems or a poor catch.

After a long discussion the association chairman John James Fullerton and its secretary Jeemie Pottinger convinced the lady that her interpretation of the rule was wrong.

An important development of 1964 was the extension of UK fishing limits to 12 miles – a move that was welcomed by Shetland fishermen. There were a few concessions for foreign fishermen who had traditionally fished in that area, such as Norwegian fishermen catching dogfish and sharks who could still fish legally up to six miles of the shore.

The growing interest in catching shellfish led to the formation of a shellfish branch of the association in April 1969. It was funded by a levy of one half pence in the pound of gross earnings and a membership fee of five shillings per boat. John James Fullerton was appointed chairman of the branch.

Its first effort was to approach the Secretary of State seeking a by-law to prohibit fishing for scallops around Shetland from the end of May to the end of September each year and a ban on scallop fishing on Saturdays and Sundays throughout the year.

The Secretary of State turned down this request since in his opinion there was no evidence that the stock was being overfished. Nevertheless the local fleet observed its own voluntary close season for a number of years.

The association lobbied hard for improved piers for shellfish boats. In January 1971 its list of priority was Symbister, Graven, Linkshouse, Skerries, Cullivoe, Vidlin, Ronas Voe and the Manor House Pier at Burravoe.

There was a remarkable degree of unanimity among the members of the association. Only once did an issue threaten to split the association. This came in the late 1960s when most of the Lerwick fishermen had abandoned the traditional weekend in favour of Friday nights ashore when the younger fishermen could have a night on the town to compensate for Sunday which they chose to spend at sea.

This was a period of heavy catches of white fish when quotas were allocated among the various boats. Fishermen from Scalloway and Burra complained that this gave the Lerwick men an unfair advantage by landing heavy catches for Monday markets. They had then been given the same quotas for Tuesday as boats that had remained ashore on Sundays.

These grievances were discussed at a special meeting on the association on 21st March, 1970. After a lengthy discussion members voted by twenty votes to nine that Sunday fishing should be discontinued.

The meeting was attended by six representatives of the processors. In a general discussion it was then agreed that boats would be allowed to fish any five nights per week, making five landings on the understanding that the quota for Monday would be the same as the quota for Friday.

CHAPTER FOUR

Changes in the herring fishery

The herring fishery enjoyed a period of stability in the late 1950s as just over 20 boats switched from seine netting to drift netting in April or May each year. In 1958 two local boats followed the example of some fishermen from North East Scotland, who "boxed" their catches in aluminium tins, counting six to the cran, and after one or two nights fishing landed them at Aberdeen.

A year later five Shetland boats were involved in this activity and by 1961 11 local boats were involved. Boxing continued throughout the season, as local merchants who started working in June preferred boxed herring to herring carried in bulk.

To find room in their holds for several hundred aluminium boxes the crews had to modify the traditional system of operation. Whereas the herring bowes had been carried in the after part of the hold, they were now carried on deck in a specially designed framework, protected by netting, on the port side of the deckhouse.

This activity affected the design of the *Dauntless II*, which arrived at Burra in March 1961 and began boxing herring in May that year. With a length of 76 feet she was designed to carry a bigger load of herring and deliver it more quickly to Aberdeen, while her hold, chilled by a Halls refrigeration system, ensured that the catch would reach the market in good condition.

Ice manufacturers J. & M. Shearer assisted this activity when in 1961 they installed a Hallmark ice plant in their premises at Garthspool, to produce flake ice, which is less damaging to herring than the conventional lumps of crushed ice.

Shooting driftnets from the Burra boat *Ocean Reaper* (skipper Geordie Hunter) off the Ramna Stacks in 1964. From left: Gideon Williamson, Sidney Simpson, Alan Halcrow, Peter Johnson, Tammie Inkster, David Williamson, Sammy Christie and William Leask.

Photo – J. R. Nicolson

Hauling the nets on the Burra boat *Golden Harvest* (skipper Jeemie Fullerton) in 1968. From left: Sidney Simpson, John David Anderson, Philip Hughes and Scottie Christie. At the rail are brothers Theo and Jimmy Fullerton, later to be skippers of the *Be Ready* and *Donvale II*. John David Anderson became the skipper of the Skerries boat *Alison Kay*. The screen of netting was used in some boats to prevent the herring from coming aft as they were shaken out of the nets.

Photo – John H. Goodlad

To add more excitement to the fishery LHD Ltd donated an annual award. It was introduced in 1957 when a pair of binoculars was presented to the boat with the highest gross earnings for herring landed at Shetland. First winner was the Whalsay boat *Serene*. The Burra boats *Venture* and *Sunshine* were the next two winners before the *Serene* won it back in 1960.

In 1961 the award was changed to a silver cup awarded for the biggest day's landing of the season. Winner that year was the Burra boat *Venture* with a fine shot of 262½ crans. The next winners were the *Orion* of Whalsay in 1962 and 1963, the *Venture* in 1964 and another Burra boat, the *Sceptre*, in 1965. By this time it had become known as the Bertie Robertson Trophy named after the company's managing director who died in 1963.

The *Serene* arriving at Lerwick on 26th July, 1960, with a huge catch of 247½ crans. Built for skipper Mackie Polson and partners she was the first of the dual purpose boats to arrive in Whalsay in post-war years. From left are: Willie Arthur, John Williamson, Thomas Anderson and Robert Anderson.

Photo – Dennis Coutts

Laying down the nets, ready to be shot again after the catch has been unloaded. The crew of the *Venture* are (from left): Joe Laurenson, John James Laurenson, Johnnie Cumming, Albert Sinclair, Alex Malcolmson, Joe Irvine and Drewie Pottinger

Photo – Dennis Coutts

The number of curing firms based at Lerwick dropped steadily throughout the 1950s. In 1963 there were only five of them at Lerwick – W. Slater & Son, Joseph Slater, Pommer & Thomsen, J. & M. Shearer and A. Wood & Sons. That was an excellent season with total landings of 43,416 crans. The curers handled 12,551 crans; a further 19,416 crans were frozen; 309 crans were kippered and 7528 crans were freshed. Freshing had resumed the previous year when the East German vessel *Von Beckerath* carried away 3056 crans. This became an important outlet as more vessels were involved.

Another change came in the early 1960s, when D. & A. MacRae of Fraserburgh hired fast fishing boats to run between Lerwick and Fraserburgh

Discharging the catch from the hold after the nets have been hauled back up to the deck, leaving the catch clear in the hold. The catch was unloaded in baskets measuring four baskets to the cran. The boat discharging at Shearers' station, Lerwick, is the *Swiftwing II* from Skerries. Those in the picture are Cecil Williamson and John William Anderson.

Photo – Magnus Shearer collection

with cargoes of herring boxed and iced in their holds. The first two were the *Spes Clara* and *Magnificent*. Those operating in 1964 were the *Morning Star* and *Coral Isle*. This continued to be an important outlet for several years, with up to six carriers operating a continuous service during the season and creating a lot of activity at both Lerwick and Scalloway. The sound of the empty tins rattling on the quays as they were thrown ashore in a frenzied haste to get them refilled and reloaded as quickly as possible, is one that no-one who heard it will ever forget.

By this time the old fashioned kippering kilns were being phased out. J. & M. Shearer had stopped working in their old kiln below the North Road at Lerwick, leaving this activity to Blair & Smith and Shetland Seafood's. At Scalloway Iceatlantic rented the old kiln at Mid Shore for a few seasons, until modern Toray kilns were installed in their premises at Blacksness.

Problems at East Anglia

The number of boats taking part in the fishery at East Anglia declined rapidly in the late 1950s. In 1958 those taking part were the *Jessie Sinclair*, *Ocean Reaper* and *Venture*. There was a break until 1962, when the *Enterprise* and *Golden Harvest* fished out of Lowestoft.

By 1963 it was clear that the fishery was in decline, with only 53 Scottish boats at Yarmouth with 21 English vessels and ten from Scotland (including the Shetland boats *Enterprise*, *Golden Harvest* and *Scotch Queen*) fished from Lowestoft. That was the last involvement by Shetland vessels in a tradition which started in 1900 with the sailboat *Swan*.

One of the reasons for the rapid decline of the driftnet fishery off East Anglia was the development of a trawl fishery for herring by fishermen in Denmark, Germany and other countries. Drifter crews were often afraid to shoot their nets, in case they were torn away by passing trawlers, the two forms of fishing being wholly incompatible.

Unlike the drifters the trawlers fished for herring at several times of the year. In Denmark herring was used in a huge industrial fishery, being converted into fish meal to feed pigs and poultry. The end of the East Anglian herring fishery was assured when Danish fishermen discovered the area where the herring, spawned off East Anglia, gathered to feed and grow. They were regarded as "trash" fish and were scooped up in large quantities, leaving fewer adults to return to the English side of the North Sea.

Landings of herring were so poor in 1965 that the organisers of the Prunier Trophy decided that there should be no presentation that year. The last year that the trophy was presented was 1966 when only 9747 crans were landed at Yarmouth and 5930 crans at Lowestoft. The trophy was won by the Fraserburgh boat *Tea Rose* for a catch of 128 crans, landed at Yarmouth. She was formerly the Lerwick fishing boat *Mary Watt*.

The threat to Shetland

For their part Shetlanders were unaware of the changes that were taking place in Norway where purse seining had developed into a highly efficient technique.

From an operation carried out by two small boats transported to the grounds on a much larger vessel, which also carried the catch ashore, the Norwegians had adopted the single boat system, which allowed a high degree of mechanisation to take place.

Important innovations of that period were the introduction of the hydraulic winch to haul the heavy purse wires to close the net, the puretic power block to haul the vast amount of netting, and the introduction of sonar to locate the shoals.

Up to 1962 the Norwegian herring catch was about 14,000 tonnes a year. In 1963, as more modern purse seiners joined the fleet, it increased to 33,000 tonnes. Then more vessels were built, old whalers and sealers were converted for purse seining and in 1964 the catch soared to 184,000 tonnes.

At first the Norwegian purse seine fleet confined its activities to the eastern side of the North Sea. The first Norwegian herring boats to be seen at Shetland were a few poorly equipped drifters, which landed their catches at Lerwick in 1964. It is now generally accepted that these were inshore boats, driven from their traditional grounds by modern methods of fishing.

In 1965 over 250 Norwegian purse seiners arrived in the waters around Shetland, following the herring shoals right up to the 12 mile limit, while a few strayed inside it, their skippers appearing in Lerwick Sheriff Court for infringing British fishing limits. During bad weather Lerwick harbour was crowded with purse seiners and local people were amazed at the size of those nets – 280 fathoms long and 70 fathoms deep – which, it was said, could cover three football pitches.

Part of the Norwegian purser fleet at anchor in Lerwick Harbour in 1965. The traditional drift netters from Scotland and Shetland can be seen lying at the quayside.

Photo – Dennis Coutts

There was resentment on the part of British drifter men as they saw the pursers shooting and hauling their nets throughout the day, catching hundreds of tons at times, whereas the drifter could set its net only once a day, for very little reward if the herring failed to come near the surface. There was resentment too that the purse seiners' catches were merely dumped into the hold of the vessel, being destined solely for the fish meal factories, instead of being handled carefully for human consumption.

There was much debate in Shetland and a few letters in the local press regarding this threat to Shetland's herring fishery. Many members of the public believed that the Herring Industry Board would take steps to prevent a similar slaughter the following year.

The Board had no power to regulate a fishery carried out in international waters. It had no wish to see the Scottish fishery ruined; but the success of the purse seine could not be denied. Moreover the UK was having to import vast quantities of fish meal for its own agricultural industry, at a time when the raw material was available on its own doorstep. It was estimated that in 1965 Norwegian vessels caught 190,000 tonnes of herring in the North Sea, compared with only 16,000 tonnes by British drifters.

Shetland Fishermen's Association showed its concern when the secretary was instructed to write to the Secretary of State for Scotland and the islands' MP Jo Grimond, urging a close investigation into the likely effects of extensive purse seining on the fishing stocks. Both promised their fullest co-operation.

Inevitably there were fishermen who realised that purse seining had become a fact of life in British waters. The first British purse seiners were the converted white fish seiner *Glenugie III* from Peterhead (skipper Donald Anderson) and the Fleetwood side trawler *Princess Anne*, both of which fished at Shetland in 1966 and proved that British fishermen could handle a purse seine as effectively as the Norwegians. They also disproved the claim that herring taken in the purse seine was unsuitable for curing.

In August that year Lerwick Town Council, disturbed by rumours that two large fish meal plants were to be built at Avoch and Fortrose, approached the Herring Industry Board with the suggestion that the Government should build a new fish meal factory at Lerwick, to handle the increased supplies of herring which they could foresee being landed at Shetland.

In an attempt to break down the suspicion of most Shetland fishermen the Shetland Council of Social Service organised film shows in Burra and Whalsay, demonstrating the type of gear required, the various steps in the fishing operation and the huge catches which could be taken by this method.

At that time a small motor boat or dory was considered essential in the fishing operation to tow the stern of the larger vessel away from the net, during the critical pursing period as the net was being closed. Some vessels engaged an older fishing vessel for this purpose, with the added benefit that she could carry part of the catch ashore. The *Glenugie*'s partner was another Peterhead vessel the *Lunar Bow*.

From the beginning there were fishermen in Shetland who realised that it was futile to try to resist a new technique. Shetland's first purse seiner, the *Adalla*, was one of three British vessels to start purse seining in 1967, the others being the Banff registered *Heritage* and the *Vigilant* from Peterhead. They were slightly larger than the typical Scottish fishing vessel of that period and had been designed with purse seining in mind.

The 92ft long *Adalla* was bought from Norway by Dr Alistair Goodlad and partners, with Thomas Milne of Peterhead as skipper. Although she had a short career in Shetland, she proved that local fishermen could master the new technique.

Another vessel of great importance to Shetland was the *Semla*, built for Salvesens of Leith. Several Shetlanders served as crewmembers, gaining valuable experience. She was ahead of her time in many ways. Her catch was pumped out of the net into refrigerated seawater tanks, taking the place of the conventional hold, and pumped ashore at the end of the trip. After a few years the *Semla* was sold to a company operating from Morocco.

In July 1967 the chairman of the Herring Industry Board George Middleton came to Shetland to urge local fishermen to invest in purse seiners and help to reduce the country's dependence on imported fish meal. He received an unfavourable response from the owners of local drifters. By this time most of them had repaid the loans on their boats and were making a reasonable living so were reluctant to change.

Although Lerwick did not get its new fish meal plant the owners of the Herring By-Products plant at Bressay decided in March 1968 to install additional equipment which would treble the output of the factory.

By this time Shetland was at the centre of an enormous industrial fishery, carried out mainly be Scandinavian vessels. In 1968 foreign vessels landed over 11,000 tons of herring for fish meal at the Bressay factory and over 9,500 tons of white fish.

The latter came from a new fishery, as far as Shetland was concerned. It was carried out by Danish vessels using small meshed nets to catch pout, a small fish whose main importance was as food for larger white fish species. Unfortunately the catches were found to contain sizeable quantities of immature and adult haddock and whiting and this caused resentment among the crews of local white fish vessels, who regarded the fishery as a threat to their livelihood. This fishery came as a result of the dramatic increase in demersal species in the North Sea in the early 1960s, as stocks of haddock, cod and whiting increased dramatically, in what scientists referred to as the "gadoid explosion". It goes without saying that the abundance of small fish to feed upon played a big part in this phenomenon.

To enable the pout fishery to proceed the British Government set a by-catch limit in 1968, allowing up to 10 per cent of "protected" species in a catch of pout. This rule was frequently broken and Danish skippers appeared regularly in Lerwick Sheriff Court. The landings at Bressay were just the tip of the iceberg, as heavy landings were made at fishmeal factories in Denmark from the Shetland area.

The first purse seiner to be built for Shetland owners was the *Wavecrest*, built at Renfrew for skipper Jim Henry and partners. Made of steel, she was 86ft long with a beam of 22.5ft and a maximum draught of 12ft. She was powered by a 425hp Caterpiller engine and was equipped with the latest navigational aids and fish finding equipment. She arrived in Shetland mid-way through the summer fishery of 1969.

Owners of the *Wavecrest*, Peter Johnson, Jim Henry, Alan Halcrow, Campbell Inkster and Jim Nicolson, celebrate her arrival at Scalloway with family and friends.

Photo – Peter Johnson

The *Wavecrest* retained the traditional dual-purpose capability, being equipped to catch white fish during the winter, a seine net winch being installed abaft the deckhouse. Another innovation was a deck shelter, which could be bolted on to the rails and whaleback to provide greater safety for crewmen gutting fish on the foredeck.

The vessel used a dory to assist in the pursing operation but soon exchanged this when the owners of the *Sunbeam* agreed to work as a partner.

In the early days of purse seining each vessel carried a supply of aluminium boxes to deliver as much of the catch as possible for human consumption. Once the bag of the net was strapped along the starboard rail, the catch was lifted out by means of a brailer at the end of a long boom and emptied into pounds on deck, from where the herring ran down through a chute to the hold.

When sea conditions were favourable it was possible to bring the help-boat alongside and swing brailerfulls of herring onto the deck of that vessel too, so that both crews were employed in boxing. When a big catch was being taken onboard there was no alternative but to stow the extra herring in partitions for'ard in the hold, separated by iron stanchions and locker boards.

The next purse seiner for Shetland owners was the steel-hulled *Serene*, built in Norway for skipper Mackie Polson and partners in Whalsay in 1969. She was followed by a wooden vessel named *Unity* for Skipper Robbie Williamson and partners, also of Whalsay. The island's third purse seiner the

Shetland's first purse seiners. From right: *Azalea*, *Wavecrest*, *Serene* and *Unity* discharge their catches into boxes on Alexandra Wharf, Lerwick.

Photo – Martin Smith

Azalea (skipper Josie Simpson) arrived in 1972 when there were 12 purse seiners in the UK fleet, four of them based in Shetland.

While curing firms still bought much of the catch, Norwegian vessels and old fishing boats from Faroe bought considerable quantities for salting onboard. They were referred to as klondykers, even though no "freshing" was involved.

These outlets could not handle the entire catch and for a large surplus the only outlet was the fish meal factory. There were times when crews went to sea knowing that their catch would be delivered to the "gut factory". On such occasions there was no attempt at boxing and some enormous catches were taken ashore. There was great concern when the *Quo Vadis*, the only purse seiner from Northern Ireland at that time, capsized south of Sumburgh Head while taking a large catch onboard in September 1970. Fortunately her crew were rescued, including Shetlander Russell Smith who was onboard at the time.

The impact of the drifters

The introduction of purse seining had little effect on the drifters for several years and they remained the dominant force in the local fishery. Twenty drifters took part in the fishery in 1966 which turned out to be the best season since 1947 with 37,416 crans worth £179,309. That was the year when catches by purse seiners first entered Shetland's fisheries statistics with 1949 crans valued at £11,575. Winner of the Bertie Robertson Trophy was the Whalsay boat *Fortuna*.

Shetland fishermen gained a valuable concession that year after the Icelandic vessel *Ellidi* had landed 800 crans for freezing. Realising that the higher prices obtained from the processing sector was the last hope for the driftermen, they received an assurance that in future all foreign landings would have to go to the fish meal factory. There was a curious distinction in that foreign landings at the fish meal factory were calculated in hundredweights – not crans.

The drifters had an even better year in 1967, when they landed 41,000 crans valued at £215,900, while the catch taken by purse seine had increased to 2700 crans valued at £17,000. The Bertie Robertson Trophy was won by the Burra boat *Scotch Queen* with a catch of 195½ crans.

The arrival of the dual purpose vessel *Korona* in 1968 showed that Peter Jamieson and his crew continued to have faith in drift netting. She won the Bertie Robertson Trophy that year and the next one. Another landmark in 1968 was the last landing by the *Research*, the last of the Zulus fishing anywhere in Scotland. Her skipper Bobby Polson was 72 and a few of his crew were also past the normal retirement age. On her last night at sea she had

The crew of the drifter *Korona* and their awards after winning the Bertie Robertson Trophy for the best catch by a drifter in 1968. Back row (from left): John Simpson, Alex Kay, Edward Anderson, Graeme Sandison, Arthur Hutchison and David Anderson. Front row (from left): Alastair Sandison, Peter Jamieson, Joe Kay Anderson and John Irvine.

Photo – Dennis Coutts

a respectable shot of 27 crans. Five curing firms were working that year and four carriers were running to Fraserburgh.

As late as 1969 the drifters were still the dominant force with 17 vessels landing 43,700 crans while the purse seiners landed 21,500 crans. There were five curing firms, including W. Slater & Sons, who joined with a Dutch firm to produce a very lightly cured herring, kept refrigerated during the journey to Holland.

That was the last good year for the drifters since it was clear that the herring stocks were becoming exhausted. The first indication that something was wrong came in 1970 when 22 drifters began the summer fishery but their

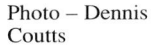

Retirement for the *Research* at the end of the 1968 herring season. It was also retirement for skipper Bobby Polson (standing on the pier) and some of his crew. On the vessel, from left: Gibbie Williamson, Willie Andrew Hughson, Tammy Simpson, Johnnie Paton, Willie Anderson, Willie Williamson, Geordie Williamson, George Magnus Leask and Willie Williamson.

Photo – Dennis Coutts

catches were far below average. By the end of July only five were still fishing. The total driftnet catch amounted to 10,198 crans whereas the catch taken by purse seine had soared to 66,787 crans. The Burra boat *Radiant Star* got her name on the Bertie Robertson Trophy for the first time.

In 1971 only three Shetland drifters fitted out for the herring fishery being joined by about 20 boats from north-east Scotland. They landed 13,893 crans from 515 arrivals while the purse seiners with 607 landings to their credit, discharged 84,638 crans. A total of 67,000 crans went for fish meal. The winner of the Bertie Robertson trophy that year and the next two years was the Burra boat *Ocean Reaper*.

In 1974 it was decided that the competition was no longer meaningful, with only two or three boats taking part in the driftnet fishery each year. Another important change took place that year when the cran measure was abolished, being replaced by a new metric measurement, the 100kg unit, roughly two thirds of a cran and measured as four aluminium tins.

Yet another change in 1974 was the action by the North East Atlantic Fisheries Commission to allocate quotas to each country taking part in the herring fishery. The UK's share was insufficient and the purse seiners had to stop fishing before the end of the year.

In 1975 the quota was even smaller – only 16,000 tonnes to be spread over two summer seasons. Close seasons were introduced and the local purse seiners turned their attention to other species, such as sprats and mackerel, or went trawling for white fish.

In 1975 the Burra boat *Replenish* was the last Shetland boat to take part in the driftnet fishery and her catches were so poor that she stopped fishing after a few weeks, bringing to an end the long history of drift netting at Shetland.

Another purse seiner joined the local fleet that year, the *Antares* for skipper Lowrie Irvine

The end of the Shetland driftnet herring fishery in 1975 and the Burra boat *Replenish* accepts the inevitable as the herring stocks are exhausted through overfishing. From left: Sam Pottinger, Robbie Christie, Lowrie Anderson, Stanley Pottinger, David Simmons, Walter Mouat, Ertie Pottinger, George William Inkster, and John Ridland. In the wheelhouse is skipper John William Pottinger.

The *Antares* arrives in Lerwick. The partners and crew are (left to right): Wilbert Anderson, George A. Anderson, Edward Anderson, Lowrie Irvine (skipper), Arthur Polson, Leonard Reid, Johnny Polson, Bobby Irvine and Dodie Williamson.

Photo – Lowrie Irvine

and partners of Whalsay. Built at Sandhaven, she was powered by a 850hp Caterpillar engine giving her a speed of 11 knots. She was the first boat in Shetland to have side thrusters installed while she was being built. By this time some of the older vessels had had side thrusters installed.

The expansion of the UK fleet of purse seiners was only a minor part of a huge international effort, which was bringing the herring stocks to the point of extinction. Spurred on by its early success, the Norwegian pelagic fleet had gone through a second stage in its development with a rise to around 500 vessels, larger than their predecessors. Similar developments had taken place in Iceland and the Faroe Islands while a fleet of Russian side trawlers had been converted into purse seiners.

The North Sea herring were now being pursued on their spawning grounds, during their annual migrations, in their overwintering areas and back to the spawning grounds. Clearly no species could withstand such a heavy rate of fishing.

It was left to the UK Government to introduce the drastic measures required. In 1976 the Fishery Limits Act had given the European Common Market the right to control the fishing industry within 200 miles of its shores, or to the median line between its neighbours, and Britain, because of its geographical position, found most of the fishing grounds within its jurisdiction.

Its first act was to impose a complete ban on fishing for herring in its part of the North Sea as from 1st January, 1977. Inevitably this brought to an end Shetland's herring processing activity, including the curing sector, which had been in decline for several years. In 1975 local firm J. & M. Shearer joined forces with Joseph Slater. The arrangement continued in 1976 when A. Wood & Sons was also in business at Lerwick. In 1977 J. & M. Shearer worked alone – and for the last time. Only 12 years after the introduction of purse seining all traces of a fish catching and fish curing system, which had survived for hundreds of years, had been swept away under the advance of modern technology.

By this time Shetland purse seiners had extended their fishing season by operating in the Minch. In 1965 two Scottish pair trawlers began fishing there and their catches were so great that the crews of ring netters and drifters refused for a time to sell their catches to any merchant who purchased trawled herring.

The pressure of success soon overcame reluctance and by 1969 a fleet of herring trawlers and the first British purse seiners were fishing there. In 1978 the Minch was closed to herring fishing, for the same reasons that had caused the closure of the North Sea.

Driftnet fishermen argued that their system of working should be excluded from the ban so that herring continued to be landed thus ensuring the continuity of markets while not endangering the stocks. The suggestion was turned down.

The ban on fishing for herring might have marked the end of Britain's experiment with purse seining had not the fleet turned its attention to another species of pelagic fish, the Atlantic mackerel, which until than had played only a minor role in Shetland's fishing industry.

It was realised that the mackerel was widely distributed around the British Isles, especially off south-west England where, for years, Cornish fishermen had made a good living using handlines.

Offshore a huge international operation was taking place, as large fleets of factory trawlers from East European countries fished for mackerel as well as demersal species. These trawlers were soon to be affected by changes in fishing regulations, as first Iceland and then other countries extended their fishing limits to 200 miles.

When in January 1977 the EEC extended its fishery limits to 200 miles East European vessels could no longer fish for mackerel off the west and south-west coasts of the UK.

The situation was watched closely by the English firm Joint Trawlers Ltd which had wide-ranging connections with the fishing industry worldwide. Through its Swedish subsidiary the firm had already carried on an extensive trade with eastern bloc countries, at a time when such activities were frowned upon by the UK Government.

Alan Leiper, managing director of Joint Trawlers, realised that following the introduction of Britain's 200 mile limit there must be a huge unsupplied market for mackerel in Eastern Europe, while at the same time the British pelagic fleet was seeking an alternative to herring.

In March 1977, at the very end of the mackerel fishery off south-west England, which by now was attracting the attention of a few Scottish pair trawlers, and causing great disquiet among Cornish handline fishermen, Joint Trawlers got permission from the UK Government for a Russian mother ship to anchor or Falmouth to take the catches of two Scottish pair trawlers for processing.

While the experiment was not a success financially, it proved that catches of mackerel could be lifted from the fishing vessels onto the deck of the factory trawler using a brailer.

A few months later, when the summer fishery started in the Minch, the company organised a transhipping operation at Ullapool, taking the catches of Scottish vessels. Before the end of the year the whole operation had switched to Falmouth and the Scottish purse seiners moved there too.

It was clear that the pelagic fishery was starting a new chapter in its history and as it developed the scale of the operation took everyone by surprise. It was clear that another bonanza of gold mining proportions was under way and it was appropriate that the old name klondyking should be applied to it.

It became obvious to Shetland purse seine fishermen that if they wished to stay in business they would have to spend long periods at sea and travel long distances in vessels that had been designed for working around Shetland. It also became clear that Shetland had not kept pace with developments in Norway. On the fishing grounds north of Scotland they encountered vessels up to 150 feet long, their working decks enclosed to give greater safety in bad weather, their hulls divided into tanks chilled by refrigerated sea water, into which the catch was pumped in and pumped out at the end of the trip. It wasn't long before all these improvements were standard features in Shetland's purse seine fleet.

A major problem for Shetland purse seine fishermen was the small size of their vessels, which made them unsuitable for year round fishing in exposed waters and reduced their profitability, since they could carry only a small catch. In the case of steel-hulled vessels like the *Wavecrest*, *Serene* and *Azalea* the problem was alleviated by sending them to shipyards in Norway or Holland to have them lengthened, being cut in two and a new section inserted amidships. This couldn't be done in the case of wooden vessels and the only solution was to replace them with steel-hulled vessels.

In November 1978 a new *Antares* arrived from Norway for skipper Lowrie Irvine. She was 106ft long and was enclosed by a shelter deck. She was the first Shetland vessel to be built with no fish room, her entire catch being carried in RSW (refrigerated sea-water) tanks.

In July 1979 the *Charisma* joined the fleet for skipper Davie Hutchison, built at Flekkefjord in Norway for the previously unheard of sum of £1.25 million. The next arrival that year was the *Altaire* for John Peter Duncan and partners, replacing the white fish vessel of that name. The new *Altaire* was 120 feet long and carried her catch in six RSW tanks.

Arrivals in 1980 were the new *Azalea* (skipper Josie Simpson), *Zephyr* (John Arthur Irvine) and *Research* (Robbie Williamson). Bought second-hand and destined for a successful stay in Whalsay was the smaller vessel *Adenia*, bought by George William Anderson and partners.

By 1979 a definite pattern had emerged which was to continue for the next four years as the Shetland fleet was away from home for most of the year. In August the boats headed for the Minch, where Ullapool became the biggest fishing port in the UK in terms of fish transhipped. It was the nearest port to the mackerel grounds and, with the wide expanse of Loch Broom, it could accommodate large numbers of East European klondykers.

By the end of October the pursers were heading for Cornwall where Falmouth became the klondyking capital of the south-west. During the mackerel season the crews were able to fly home for long weekends, often chartering an aircraft to take them direct to Sumburgh.

Clearly this was not an ideal situation and there was considerable relief when the North Sea fishery reopened in 1983 and, to everyone's delight, the seven year ban had had the desired effect of allowing the herring stocks to recover.

The situation was entirely different from that of the early 1970s when the herring stocks had been almost annihilated during a mad free-for-all, for which all those responsible for organising the fishery must accept blame. Under the new system of management there would be total allowable catches and national quotas, fixed by international agreement, and a licensing scheme to prevent an uncontrolled expansion of the fleet

CHAPTER FIVE

The challenge from oil

In the mid-1960s, when purse seiners and trawlers were causing concern among the crews of herring drifters, another type of craft, the seismic survey vessel, was moving into the area around Shetland.

These ships were not interested in the fish stocks or in the seabed, but in the nature of the rocks that lay below the bottom of the sea, especially those that could conceivably contain oil and gas.

They had considerable success off East Anglia, where not many years before the herring men had gathered for their autumn fishery. New names appeared on the charts of the area as gas fields like Leman, Hewitt and Indefatigable were discovered and Great Yarmouth suddenly became the centre for North Sea oil and gas exploration.

As the drilling rigs moved north far more exciting finds were made – the Montrose field east of Peterhead and the Forties oil and gas field east of Buchan Ness. Almost overnight Aberdeen became the focus of international attention.

By 1970 exploration work had spread to waters east of Shetland and in July 1971 the rig Staflo, drilling a well for Shell-Esso 125 miles east of Shetland, discovered what is now the giant Brent oilfield. As usual the oil companies involved in the discovery did not reveal information about the find until they were ready to do so. For a year longer the people of Shetland were unaware of the wealth that lay over the horizon and the impact that it would have on their lives.

The oil companies were aware that Shetland was the nearest land to the oilfields of the East Shetland Basin and the obvious landfall for the pipelines that would eventually bring the oil ashore.

Zetland County Council was totally unprepared for oil-related developments but acted quickly to rectify the omission under its chief executive Ian Clark. A development plan was drawn up, which identified the area around Sullom Voe as the most suitable site for the massive complex which would receive the oil from the pipelines and prepare it for shipment to refineries in the UK and elsewhere. In addition to a vast stretch of semi-derelict land it had the advantage of a good approach via Yell Sound and sufficient depth of water to allow large oil tankers to berth at the jetties which would have to be built. By this time Yell Sound had become the centre of a lucrative fishery for shellfish. It is not surprising that scallop fishermen viewed these impending changes with considerable alarm.

The council promoted a Provisional Order seeking unique powers of control over Shetland's coastal areas. In January 1972 Shetland Fishermen's Association lodged objections to certain of the powers being sought by the council; and in June and July that year representatives of the association appeared before the Select Committee dealing with the Zetland County Council Bill.

The council achieved most of its aims, which were embodied in the Zetland County Council Act, which received the Royal Assent on 10th April, 1974. The council was given jurisdiction as port and harbour authority over Sullom Voe; the right to issue licences to dredge and to construct works within the three-mile limit, outside the areas controlled by the independent harbour authorities at Lerwick, Scalloway and Broonies Taing (Sandwick); and powers to establish a reserve fund from deals made with the oil industry. These powers passed automatically to Zetland County Council's successor, Shetland Islands Council, which was established following the reorganisation of local government in 1975.

Among the concessions won by Shetland Fishermen's Association was the stipulation that scallop beds within the three-mile limit should not be disturbed by developments without prior consultation.

A number of bodies were set up to monitor the environment around Sullom Voe and to ensure that as little harm as possible was done to local wildlife, including the marine environment. Representatives of the association were appointed to the Shetland Oil Terminal Environmental Advisory Group (SOTEAG) and to the Zetland Harbour Advisory Committee (ZHAC).

The first formal agreement between the council and the oil companies was signed in June 1974 when the latter agreed to make disturbance payments of £1.3 million to the council. On 21st April, 1975, the Sullom Voe Association was formed between the council and the oil companies BP and Shell to operate the port of Sullom Voe. This paved the way for enormous sums of money to be paid into a reserve fund. This would be used for a variety of purposes, including the promotion of local industries of which fishing and fish processing were recognised as having the greatest potential for development.

The Norwegian seismic survey vessel *Longva II* at Scalloway on 24th September, 1975. The fishing boats berthed on the opposite side of the breakwater are (from left): *Welfare*, *Milky Way* and *Venture*.

Photo – Robert Johnson

Harbour projects

In the early years of activity in the area around Shetland oil-related vessels had to compete with fishing vessels for berthage at existing piers. The biggest dispute between the two sectors came at Scalloway, where Blacksness Pier Trust leased part of the pier to Nautical Services (Shetland) Ltd., which in 1972 had won a contract from Esso Norway Inc. to provide a supply of drilling mud, chemicals and drill water for a rig operating west of Shetland.

This led to a bitter confrontation with local fishermen who pointed out that the pier had been funded by the Scottish Office from its fishing harbours budget. Under pressure most of the Trust's Executive Committee resigned, being replaced largely by fishermen.

The new committee then drew up plans for a major development to cater for both fishing and oil-related craft along the west side of the East Voe of Scalloway; but most fishermen still protested that the space proposed for their activities was totally inadequate.

Fishermen in Burra began a campaign for a new pier to the north of the bridge at Lang Sound – one of two bridges completed in October 1971 linking the islands of Burra and Trondra to the Mainland of Shetland. The Lang Sound proposal was abandoned when the problems at Scalloway were overcome.

Plans for a major oil base at Scalloway were premature since the main oilfield developments were taking place to the east of Shetland and Lerwick was the obvious place for supply bases. Nevertheless the scheme proposed for Scalloway was the impetus for major fishing and commercial developments carried out by Shetland Islands Council, after it had acquired the pier at Scalloway in 1977. As part of the agreement Blacksness Pier Trust rescinded its constitution, being replaced by a joint committee to oversee the construction of the required developments and the running of the harbour.

A supply base was established by Hudsons at Broonies Taing, where a pier to accommodate sailing drifters had been constructed in the early part of the century. The base closed after a few years, leaving an extended jetty which would be used occasionally by fishing vessels working to the south of Shetland.

Several other oil-related projects were mooted – at Ronas Voe, Basta Voe and Baltasound – but none of these came to fruition. A small jetty had been built at Ronas Voe in 1969 for the use of fishing boats operating in that area. It did not bring in much revenue and was sold to the Northmavine Fish Processing Company in 1973 for £500, on the understanding that it would be for the use of all Shetland vessels working there.

Lerwick Harbour Trust had several schemes in mind in the late 1960s. The white fish market was far too small for the heavy landings of that period so plans were drawn up for a much larger building on land to be reclaimed north of Alexandra Wharf.

The trustees also had to cater for impending changes in sea transport, with a terminal for the new Bressay ferry at Alexandra Wharf and a much larger terminal for the roll-on roll-off cargo/passenger vessel which would replace the crane-loading *St Clair*.

Fortunately land was available in the North Harbour as Bremner's herring station and Shetland Seafoods' property at Dunbar's station were both for sale. In 1971 steps were taken to purchase both properties and the land between them. That was before news broke of major oil-related developments east of Shetland and the trust realised that it would have to cater for the needs of that industry too.

In this case the trust had a stroke of luck when it negotiated successfully to purchase the Gremista Estate, a large tract of land along the west shore of the North Harbour and extending westwards as far as Dales Voe.

Having secured this valuable asset the trust then leased land for the giant supply base of Norscot Services at Gremista and for the smaller base at Holmsgarth used jointly be Shell and BP. A base outwith the trust's jurisdiction was set up jointly by Hay & Company (Lerwick) Ltd in partnership with Ocean Inchcape Ltd on land at the North Ness.

The trust went ahead with the reclamation of land between Alexandra

Wharf and the Malakoff slipway throughout 1972 and by the following summer the large quay wall was complete. The fish market was the last part of the scheme to be completed after careful consideration of present and future needs. In August 1973 it was decided that the building shown on the original plan would be far too small, so it was decided to add an extra 16 metres making it 53m long.

As early as March 1969 it had been agreed that a net repair loft should be incorporated in the upper storey of the building. It was leased to LHD Ltd who had acquired the business of D. & A. Duthie, who for several years had operated a net repair business on the first floor of a wooden building at the south end of Alexandra Wharf.

The fish market was ready in March 1975 and a few weeks later it was opened officially when retired fisherman John West cut a tape to unveil the commemorative plaque. Mr West had been a successful skipper between the wars in the steam drifters *Girl Joey* and *Maud Evelyn*. After the war he had fished as skipper of the motor boat *Blossom* and later acquired an ex-Admiralty MFV which was renamed *John West*.

Retired fisherman John West.

Photo – Robert Johnson

In August 1975 the fish market quay was given the official name of Laurenson Quay in memory of Arthur Laurenson (senior) who had served as clerk to the trust from 1938 to 1968.

Business opportunities

The discovery of oil was greeted initially with resentment on the part of many people in Shetland who recognised the transformation in the islands' economy due to fishing and fish processing since the war. A comment often heard was: "Shetland doesn't need oil. We have our fishing industry."

The business sector was quick to recognise the benefits that could come from oil and there was a spate of reorganisation, even among firms which had long been connected with the fishing industry.

At Scalloway William Moore & Sons had begun to cater for the bigger vessels joining Shetland's fishing fleet by building a new slipway adjacent to the Prince Olav slipway. Jack Moore had taken into partnership his younger son John, a promising engineer. Sadly John was drowned in a diving accident in February 1972 and the continuity in the family business which Jack Moore had hoped for was gone. Two years after John's death the business was sold to the John Wood group of Aberdeen.

About the same time Moore's' counterpart in Lerwick, the Malakoff, became part of the Lithgows Holdings (Ltd) of Glasgow. The management of the two firms decided that a working arrangement between the two companies would enable them to provide a better service to the local industry, working as Malakoff & Moore.

Both yards derived a great deal of work from the oil industry as did a new company HNP Ltd, which had started at Lerwick in 1969 as a partnership of three engineers – Hughie Hughson, Davie Nicolson and John Pottinger.

Following the end of herring curing J. & M. Shearer began to look for new opportunities. By this time Magnus J. Shearer had succeeded his father Magnus M. Shearer as managing director. The firm had already undergone a change of ownership when in 1970 it became a wholly owned subsidiary of

Herring By-Products Ltd while retaining the original management. It continued to develop, becoming involved in shipping services and attracting a considerable amount of oil-related business. In 1972 it had acquired the long established firm of Thomas W. Laurenson.

In 1984 the parent firm Herring By-Products Ltd decided to concentrate on the production of fish meal and oil and the component parts of J. & M. Shearer were sold off. The shipping service was bought by John Smith of Lerwick as Shearer Shipping Services; the engineering section was bought by Sandy Laurenson and Laurence Mullay as L. & M. Engineering; and the ice-making section was sold to Magnus J. Shearer who renamed it J. & M. Shearer (Ice Supplies) Ltd. A year later it became part of the LHD group with Mr Shearer remaining as managing director.

The impact of oil

The main development of this period was the construction of the giant oil terminal at Calback Ness – designed to handle half the oil consumption of the UK – and the loading jetties, navigational equipment and lighthouses required to convert a stretch of rocky foreshore and heather-covered moorland into the biggest oil terminal in Europe. Construction began in February 1975 and the workforce increased steadily to a peak of over 7000 in 1980, two years after the first oil had been shipped out. The terminal has a throughput design capacity of 1.41 million barrels of crude oil per day – the equivalent of 70 million tonnes per year.

During all this hectic activity boats still fished for crabs, lobsters and scallops in Yell Sound, using the tiny jetty at Graven as their base, accepting the passage of large cargo ships bringing in construction materials, just as they would learn to co-exist with huge oil tankers.

Elsewhere the problems faced by fishermen were more acute, although Shetland Islands Council tried very hard to keep the industry informed of what was taking place. On 23rd February, 1974, members of Shetland Fishermen's Association met John Manson, the council's assistant on oil developments, to hear of the implications for the industry of what was taking place offshore. It was agreed that the association should appoint representatives to liaise with the oilmen for the benefit of both industries.

Members of the committee were Davie Anderson and Willie Simpson representing Whalsay; Jim H. Henry and Geordie Hunter (Burra); Jackie Hughson (Skerries); Jim Smith (North Isles); Jeemie Robb and Ian Watt (Scalloway); Lynn Duncan and John Scott (Lerwick); and John Peter Duncan (Northmavine). The association chairman and the local director of the Scottish Fishermen's Organisation (SFO) – which Shetland fishermen had joined following Britain's entry into the Common Market – would be ex-officio members. At that time Jeemie Wiseman and Davie Smith held these posts.

In their dealings with the fishing industry the oil companies got off to an unfortunate start due to the practice by some operators of dumping rubbish on the seabed. In part this was due simply to carelessness, in part due to a lack of understanding as regards fishing methods. It was galling for a crew to haul a net and find the codend full of old safety helmets or perforated oil drums. A more serious loss occurred when a net got snagged in an obstruction on the seabed.

A new Dumping at Sea Act, which came into force on 27th June, 1974, made it illegal to dump anything but waste water, food waste, sewage and drill cuttings without a licence to do so.

A circular was sent to all members of the UK Offshore Operators

Association pointing out that all other waste material must be transported ashore for disposal. The Act applied to the fishing industry too, since a piece of synthetic netting floating on the sea can be just as dangerous as an obstruction on the seabed.

The first real clash with the oil industry came when the route to be taken by the pipeline from the Brent and Cormorant fields was being planned. The proposed route was outlined at a special meeting when representatives of Shetland Fishermen's Association, Shetland Islands Council and other interested parties met representatives of Shell in the Fishermen's Mission at Lerwick on 11th May, 1974.

A major contribution to the discussion was made by David B. Craig of the Scottish Trawlers Federation, who pointed out that the proposed route would cut across some of the most productive fishing grounds in the Shetland area as it passed to the east of Fetlar and south of Yell. He also feared pollution and damage to fishing gear during and after the pipe-laying operation.

Shell's representatives were asked why the pipeline should not be diverted away from those fishing areas and laid south of Out Skerries. They replied that this route had not been surveyed. They agreed to carry out a survey and requested that in the meantime preparatory work should be allowed to go ahead near the proposed landfall at Firths Voe.

The fishermen present said that they had no objection to this and added an additional plea that if it was found impracticable to lay the pipeline south of Out Skerries it should be laid no more than one mile north of the group and should run south of the Pobie Bank.

At the next meeting with representatives of the oil companies on 23rd August, 1974, fishermen were told that it had been found impracticable to lay a pipeline south of the Pobie Bank and south of Out Skerries. There was no alternative to a route through the fishing grounds; but every possible effort would be made to minimise disturbance.

An ad hoc committee was set up to deal with the anticipated claims and complaints from the fishing industry. It consisted of representatives from Shetland Fishermen's Association, the Sea Fisheries Inspectorate, the pipeline operators, the UK Offshore Operators Association, the Scottish Trawlers Federation and Shetland Islands Council, to deal with the expected claims and complaints from the fishing industry.

Preparations for laying the pipeline began in 1974, the first visible sign of activity being a number of large steel buoys anchored in Yell Sound, constituting a hazard to shipping after dark since they were unlit. There was also friction as oil-related vessels claimed priority at local piers such as Tofts Voe and Graven.

The oil companies realised that good relations with the fishermen were of crucial importance and that their activities were bound to cause inconvenience to the fishing industry. In February 1975 Shell agreed to make an ex gratia payment to Shetland Fishermen's Association of £25,000, within one month of the start of pipe-laying in the vicinity of Firths Voe, "in consideration of the temporary disturbance of laying and burying the 36 inch diameter pipeline on fishing grounds around Shetland."

The company also agreed to minimise the disturbance by publishing weekly bulletins giving information as to the location of construction hazards, in *The Shetland Times* and *Fishing News* and also to inform the Coastguard, the Hydrographer of the Royal Navy and the radio services of the Department of Agriculture & Fisheries for Scotland.

BP followed suit with a payment to the association of £45,000 for disturbance caused in laying its pipeline from the Ninian field to its landfall at Grutwick on the east side of Lunna Ness. The association decided that these

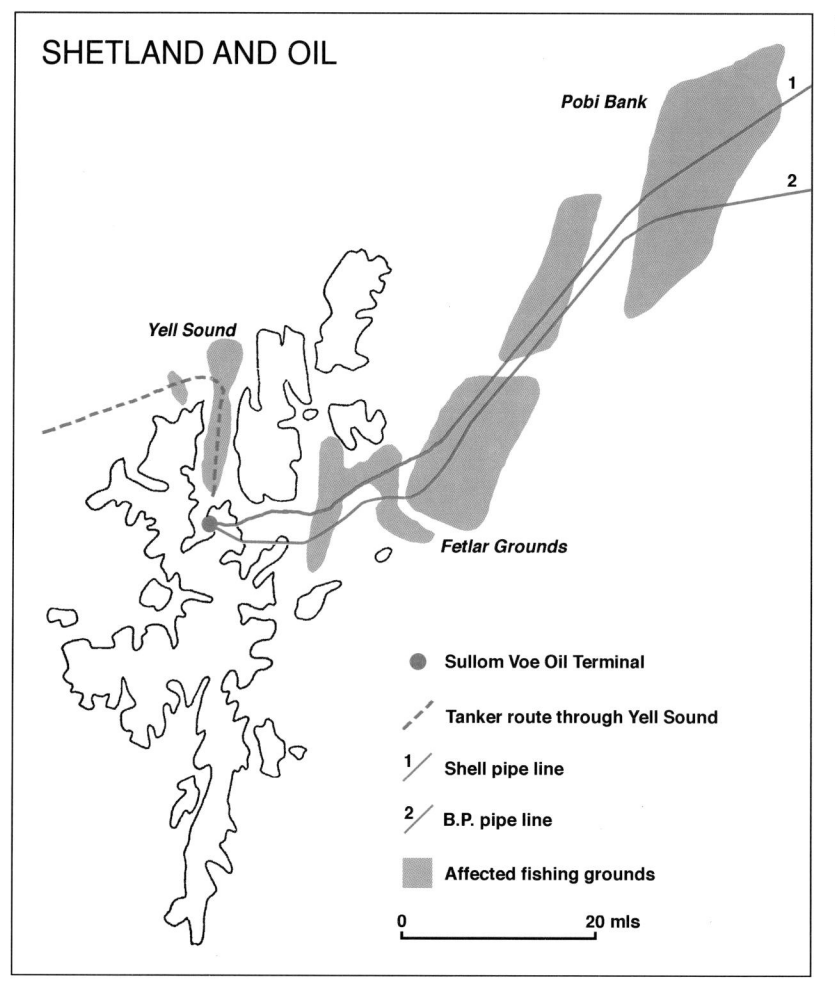

SHETLAND AND OIL

Pobi Bank

1

2

Yell Sound

Fetlar Grounds

● Sullom Voe Oil Terminal

Tanker route through Yell Sound

1 Shell pipe line

2 B.P. pipe line

Affected fishing grounds

0   20 mls

Fishing and oil.

payments should form the basis of a special fund to provide loans to young fishermen. Shetland Islands Council decided to match the donations from the oil companies and the Shetland Fishermen's Trust was set up in 1975 with capital of £140,000. Having negotiated the early compensation payment from the oil industry, a more confident association swiftly secured a further £25,000 from the oil terminal operators in 1979. This 'one-off payment' was in respect of lost shellfish grounds resulting from the building of a ballast water treatment plant into the sea at Sullom Voe.

There were times when fishermen felt that the oil companies had got off lightly. As deep trenches were dug on the seabed, prior to burying the pipes, huge boulders were brought to the upper layer of the seabed and these caused a lot of damage to fishing gear when caught in the wings or codend of a trawl or seine net. Just as damaging to fishing gear were the huge mounds of clay and gravel left by the anchors as the pipe-laying barge crawled along the route of the pipeline.

The local purse seiner/trawler *Wavecrest* (skipper Jim Henry) was given a contract to trawl along the track of the pipeline, removing obstacles which might damage the fishing gear.

There were problems with the pipelines themselves as the concrete coating broke off in places, resulting in damage to nets. There was also the embarrassing situation when part of the pipeline floated in Yell Sound after all its protective coating had been shed. This section was re-laid on the seabed, being anchored by means of concrete "saddles".

Fishermen were told that while it should be possible to trawl over the pipelines, whose routes were carefully marked on new charts of the area, there was always the possibility that fishing gear could get caught in the coating. Should that happen it was essential that fishermen should not use force to free the net but should cut their gear to avoid causing damage to the pipeline.

The oil companies agreed that compensation would be paid by the owners of the pipeline concerned to any vessel whose owners could prove that they had sacrificed a net to avoid damage. A committee was set up to speed up the settlement of such claims. Among its members was a representative of Shetland Fishermen's Association.

With reluctance Shetland fishermen had to accept the fact that the laying of the pipelines had caused permanent damage to some of the best fishing grounds to the north-east of Shetland. The far Balta ground had been cut in two, the southern part virtually useless for fishing, and the Balta Broo had also been badly affected.

There were more problems for the fishermen when large oil tankers began to call at Sullom Voe, using the area to the north of Yell Sound to heave to as they waited their turn to enter Sullom Voe. Trawlers and seiners working in this area had to be extremely vigilant, ready to alter course whenever a large tanker bore down on them.

Local strains and stresses

While the herring fishery was showing signs of extinction in the 1970s the sea around Shetland was teeming with all species of white fish, feeding on dense shoals of smaller fish, including pout, which formed the basis of a huge industrial fishery by Danish vessels.

By the 1960s Danish fishermen were catching pout on both sides of Shetland in small wooden boats, usually painted blue, with a crew of only three or four men since no gutting was required in this fishery. After three or four days fishing they were ready to return home, their holds full of pout and other species taken as a by-catch.

The small wooden boats were replaced in the 1970s by large steel-hulled vessels, capable of carrying bigger catches of pout to fish meal plants in Denmark or landing their catches at the Bressay plant.

The extent of this industrial fishery caused anger among many Shetland fishermen. Others argued that if the Danes were allowed to derive a good income from a fishery off Shetland local fishermen should get a share of it too and they began to install trawl winches in their vessels.

The local fishery started in 1972 with a catch of 513 tonnes by Shetland vessels and reached its peak in 1974 with a catch of 9274 tonnes. However there was concern at the high by-catch of more important species; and involvement by the Shetland boats declined steadily until 1980 when they landed only 30 tonnes of pout.

In the meantime Shetland fishermen had turned their attention to another species, the sand eel, which had been fished commercially in other parts of the North Sea since the 1960s. The local fishery started in 1974 with a catch of 8000 tonnes and rose rapidly to a peak of 52,600 tonnes in 1982.

The success of the local sand eel fishery caused concern among crews who fished with seine nets on inshore grounds in the summer months. They pointed out that it was the abundance of sand eels that attracted shoals of large haddock to places like Mousa Sound and the South Sand off Lerwick.

The white fish sector remained important to the local economy although most processors suffered from a shortage of labour because of the higher wages being paid at Sullom Voe and other construction sites. The local markets remained the most important outlet for Shetland fishermen although several crews were still "tripping" to Aberdeen at times, especially when there was a glut of fish and boats were operating to strict quotas.

Iceatlantic was still the main year round buyer of white fish. During the 1960s, in spite of its enormous output, it had often suffered from cash flow problems and frequent changes in the post of manager. In 1969 the HIDB invested heavily in the factory and employed Captain Alex Simpson from Lerwick as manager. Under his supervision the factory enjoyed the most profitable period in its history. Another change came in 1972 when Gordon Davidson, a fish merchant from Glasgow, became a major shareholder and eventually the firm's managing director.

Scalloway received a boost in 1973 with the building of the first section of a cold store to hold consignments of frozen fish from processing plants all over Shetland, waiting to be shipped to the USA where the demand for frozen fillets remained strong.

Fishermen took a calculated risk in 1972 when they asked the processors for a price increase of one shilling (5p) on the minimum prices for haddock and whiting, otherwise they would return to the old system of sales by auction, with minimum prices as set by the White Fish Authority for Aberdeen.

A meeting between the association and representatives of the fish merchants was held in the Fishermen's Mission at Lerwick when the processors warned that if the increase was implemented many firms would go out of business.

With a considerable amount of trepidation the fishermen carried out their stated aim of returning to fish selling by auction. Fears that the merchants would boycott the sales and that the prices would drop proved groundless as the average price at local markets more than doubled within the next few years.

In 1971 the catch by seine net boats landed locally amounted to 282,700 cwt valued at £833,200, an average price of £2.94 per cwt, whereas in 1973, the first full year of the reintroduced auction system, 160,979 cwts landed locally fetched £1,222,531 – an average of £7.59 per cwt.

Another important change came in 1973 with the decision to introduce metric weights using plastic boxes holding 40kg of fish plus ice. The new boxes had the advantage of being easier to clean than the old fashioned wooden boxes.

With highly paid jobs available ashore some fishermen were tempted to leave the fishing industry for a few years, while the situation in the processing was becoming serious. With fewer workers to handle the catch there was a drop in demand leading to reduced prices at local markets.

The situation improved in 1977 when P & O Scottish Ferries introduced its new roll-on roll-off ferry service operating from Holmsgarth and merchants in Aberdeen were given ready access to Shetland markets, through their local agents, with the result that prices rose considerably, especially for top quality fish.

The early years of the oil era saw a transformation in the local fishing fleet as a number of old boats were sold outwith Shetland, their loss being offset by the arrival of new or good second hand boats. Those sold between 1971 and 1975 included the Burra boats *Brighter Dawn, Maid of the Mist, Golden Harvest, Scarlet Thread* and *Ocean Reaper*; the Scalloway boats *Evangeline,*

Golden West and *Planet*; the Lerwick boats *Fertile* and *Day Dawn* and the Skerries boats *St Clair* and *Swiftwing II*.

An arrival in 1971 was the *Comet*, built at Flekkefjord in Norway for Jackie L. Hughson and partners of Skerries. Additions in 1972 were the 76ft long *Sirius*, built at Flekkefjord for Ralph Pottinger and partners of Burra, and the *Madalia*, a wooden vessel with a transom stern for Alastair Thomason and partners of Cullivoe. Older boats bought that year were the *Elysian* (Kenneth Pottinger), *North Star* (Jim Williamson) and *Avrella* (Duncan Cumming) all of Burra, and the *Freedom* for Ivor Duncan of Lerwick.

Madalia at Scalloway, leaving the slipway of William Moore & Son after a paint-up.

Photo – Robert Johnson

The Burra boat *Elysian*, a fine example of a white fish trawler in the early 1970s.

Photo – James A. Pottinger

A further five boats joined the fleet in 1973, the most revolutionary of which was the 50ft long *Harvest Gold*, built for Robbie Watt of Lerwick. She was built in Orkney – the first boat in Shetland to have a hull of glass reinforced plastic – at a cost of £48,000.

The equipment in her wheelhouse showed the advances made for a boat of this size – a Kelvin Hughes type 17 radar, a Decca Mk 12 navigator, an Atlas 420 echosounder, a Sailor M/F radio and VHF radio communications. On deck she had a Mastra seine net/trawl winch with the still familiar Beccles coiler.

Other arrivals that year were the *Glorieuse St Therese*, a French built vessel for Russell Smith of Burra, the *Provider* for Brian Watt of Scalloway, the *Janese Watt* for James Watt of Lerwick and the inshore fishing vessel *Wings of the Morning* for Albert Wiseman of Lerwick.

1974 saw two additions to the Whalsay fleet – *Athena* (Magnie Jamieson) and *Victory* (Ronnie Hutchison). The *Constellation* arrived at Skerries for Tom Anderson and partners, the *Planet* was bought by John Umphray and partners of Scalloway and the *Brighter Morn*, originally based at Whalsay, was bought by John Garriock and partners from the Skeld area from its previous owners John Peter Duncan and partners.

Two important additions to the Whalsay fleet in 1975 were the *Venturous* (Willie Williamson) and the *Adonis* a 75ft long steel-hulled vessel built at Campbeltown for Magnie Stewart.

There was still a number of 70ft long dual purpose vessels in the local fleet and these were modernised by having a whaleback added to give more shelter for the crew when working on deck. Thulecraft of Lerwick fabricated a large number of these devices from GRP and they were attached to the vessels by Malakoff and Moore.

While seine netting was still important, trawling was steadily ousting the traditional method of catching white fish and a power block situated aft was becoming a standard fitting on both seiners and trawlers – even on the older vessels.

The crew of the Burra boat *Sceptre* gutting fish at Scalloway. In the picture, from the left, are skipper Tommy Fullerton, Maxie Williamson and Wilbert Fullerton.

Photo – Martin Smith

The association in the early 1970s

The frequency of meetings held by Shetland Fishermen's Association in the early 1970s indicates the additional work that had to be carried out by the secretary and the chairman due to oil-related matters and the steadily growing impact of the Common Market.

Josie Simpson, skipper of the Whalsay boat *Good Tidings*, served as chairman from 1969 to 1971 when he was succeeded by Bobby Peterson from Brae, skipper of the *Concord*. Jeemsie Ward from Burra, skipper of the seine netter *Unison* served from 1972 to 1973 when he was succeeded by Jeemie Wiseman of Lerwick, skipper of the inshore seine netter *Nil Desperandum*.

A bag of sprats is hoisted onboard the *Brighter Morn*, then owned by skipper John Garriock and partners. She was pair trawling with the *Pescoso* in the late 1970s.

Photo – Ewan Mowat

Throughout this period Jeemie Pottinger continued to serve as association secretary.

In addition to oil-related issues the question of better harbours was raised at numerous meetings. One of the main issues at this time was the state of the privately owned pier at Voe. This led to a reappraisal of fishing piers in the West Mainland and at one time it was agreed that the industry would be served better by a pier at Aith. This issue was settled in 1974 when repairs were carried out to the jetty at Voe, which continued to by the main landing centre for vessels working in St Magnus Bay, while small shellfish boats continued to use the small pier at West Burrafirth.

There was also the question of better facilities at Scalloway to cater for the bigger vessels now joining the local fleet and to provide better shelter with south-westerly gales. Impetus was given to this debate by the dispute between fishing and oil interests at Blacksness Pier. At one stage the association withdrew from the controversy by giving its support for the proposed new harbour at Lang Sound. On 4th August, 1975, it stated its list of priorities as Lang Sound, Ronas Voe, Voe and Uyeasound.

Fishermen in other areas felt that their problems should be given greater attention. In June 1974 a petition signed by 15 fishermen in Cullivoe was sent to Zetland County Council, who forwarded it to the association for its comments. The problem there was insufficient depth of water so that boats moored at the pier were bumping the seabed at low tide.

In April 1975 a petition signed by 150 fishermen in Whalsay sought the support of the association for a breakwater in the North Voe because of sever congestion in the existing harbour. This was caused by larger vessels joining the island's fleet and also the space required for the new roll-on roll-off ferry.

The issue of industrial fishing was raised at numerous meetings of the association – especially the pout fishery now being carried on extensively by large trawlers from Denmark, Norway and Faroe.

On 18th May, 1974, at a meeting of the executive committee, attended also by representatives of the fish merchants association, skipper Davie Smith drew attention to a decline in white fish stock west of Shetland, which in his opinion was due to intensive fishing for pout and the huge by-catch of edible species. The secretary was instructed to write to the Department of Agriculture and Fisheries to ask for a complete ban on pout fishing in a conservation area which should be established west of Shetland.

A map of the area proposed was published in *The Shetland Times*, together with the reasons for seeking such a ban, and members of the public were invited to come forward with any objections which they might have to the proposal. No objections to the plan came from Shetland.

This attempt at conservation failed when the Department of Agriculture and Fisheries turned down the request, pointing out that the UK Government had no jurisdiction over foreign vessels engaged in an industrial fishery on the high seas. Furthermore a considerable amount of scientific research had been carried out on the impact of industrial fishing for pout and other species and there was no evidence to suggest that these fisheries had a detrimental effect on commercial stocks.

The Government was convinced that it had done all it could to regulate this fishery when, in 1968, it introduced its new Immature Sea Fish Order which provided for a limit of no more than 10 per cent by weight of immature white fish to be landed by industrial trawlers. It was clear to Shetland fishermen glancing in the holds of industrial trawlers berthed at Lerwick or discharging their catches at the Bressay fish meal plant that this figure was often exceeded by a wide margin.

Further representation came from Shetland in 1975 when a heavy concentration of Danish, Norwegian and Faroese vessels was spotted north of Foula and off Unst. The Department reiterated the view that this issue must be tackled at a international level. It reminded Shetland fishermen that industrial landings by Scottish vessels had reached a figure of around one million cwts worth £1.6 million in 1974 compared with 500,000 cwts worth £1 million in 1973. It also pointed out that in 1974 industrial landings at Lerwick amounted to 550,000 cwts worth £890,000. The communication did not explain that most of this catch came from foreign vessels.

CHAPTER SIX

Shetland and the Common Market

Shetland fishermen were blissfully unaware of the implications for their industry of moves made in 1951 when France, West Germany, Italy, Belgium, the Netherlands and Luxembourg set up the European Coal and Steel Community. Few realised at the time that this was the first step in a movement towards European unity.

On 25th March, 1957, the six countries signed the Treaty of Rome, under which they agreed to establish the European Economic Community or Common Market, which came into being on 1st January, 1958.

Agriculture was important in all of these countries and it was decided to harmonise that industry throughout the member states with a Common Agricultural Policy which was set up in 1962.

None of these countries had much to offer in the way of fish stocks and it was only when the UK, Denmark and Ireland applied to join the Common Market that the idea of a Common Fisheries Policy began to take hold, the framework for this being in place when these countries joined the Common Market in January 1973.

From the very beginning of negotiations with Europe Shetland fishermen were anxious about the implications for the future of the industry. By that time six original members of the EEC were talking about the removal of all fishing limits and full access by fishermen of one country to the waters of all member states. Anxiety was heightened among British inshore fishermen when the Cameron report proposed that the restrictions on trawling and seine netting within three miles of the shore should be removed.

In an attempt to make it easier for British fishermen to accept the terms for UK membership of the EEC it was agreed that for a period of 10 years after Britain's accession to the EEC the 12 mile limit would remain in place.

On 5th February, 1970, the executive committee of Shetland Fishermen's Association met to discuss the conditions for Britain's entry as negotiated by Geoffrey Ripon. The meeting decided to write to the Department of Agriculture and Fisheries for Scotland, stating that while Shetland welcomed the continuation of the 12 mile limit for 10 years, it wanted an assurance that no effort would be spared by those in authority at the expiry of the transitional period to extend the UK fisheries limit to 25 miles from the shore.

In December 1970 the association's chairman Josie Simpson and its secretary Jeemie Pottinger were in London for discussions on the effects on the inshore fishing industry if Britain joined the EEC.

A few months later Mr Simpson was one of a small group from Orkney and Shetland who visited Denmark, Germany, Belgium, Italy, Sweden, Switzerland and Norway, the trip being organised by the local Conservative party. Mr Simpson said that one of the most encouraging aspects of the tour was to find small businesses co-existing quite happily with large concerns in all these countries.

The promise of a ten-year transitional period for UK fishermen did little to allay the fears of local people, as was shown in the correspondence columns of *The Shetland Times*. In a lengthy article in the issue of 5th February, 1971, Development Officer Mike Stansbury concluded: "The most serious principle as far as Shetland is concerned is the removal of the fishing limits and the consequent loss in time of our fishing stock."

The newspaper's editor Basil Wishart, after spending three days at the headquarters of the EEC, wrote: "Britain will become a member of the EEC. She will do so despite disadvantages which are likely to include the reduction of fishing limits from 12 miles to six; and Norway is unlikely to join because she regards a 12 mile limit as essential for the welfare of her inshore fishermen."

Britain became a full member of the EEC on 1st January, 1973. On 24th February, the association secretary explained to his members how the system of Producer Organisations would work. Fish would continue to be sold on the open market; but there would now be pre-determined withdrawal prices, based on "guide" prices calculated from market prices over the previous three years.

It was suggested that Shetland was too small an area to have its own PO and that it should seek membership of the Scottish Fishermen's Organisation. First local director of the Organisation was Jeemsie Ward, replaced soon afterwards by Davie Smith, who was joined by Geordie Hunter and Jeemie Wiseman. Additional directors appointed on 18th May, 1974, were Norman Poleson, Magnus Henry, Jackie Hughson and John Scott.

Shetland Fishermen's Association also became a member of the Scottish Fishermen's Federation, a national body representing all the fishermen of Scotland. Set up in the autumn of 1973, its immediate purpose was to negotiate on behalf of all its members the best possible deal in the renegotiation of the Common Fisheries Policy.

In January 1975 Shetland fishermen took the first step in organising their affairs within the SFO when they fixed withdrawal prices for three grades of haddock and four grades of cod and their own regional price structure for four grades of whiting.

The scheme got off to a bad start in September 1975 as processors claimed that they had not been consulted about the new fixed minimum prices and claimed that the minimum prices set for small haddock were too high. To show their feelings they refused to buy small haddock and in the first two days of the new system a total of 4200 cwts remained unsold and were sent to the fish meal plant at Bressay.

It was a new experience for fishermen to receive a minimum price set by the PO for those fish, paid by the EEC, instead of the low prices paid by the fish meal manufacturer.

Nevertheless they were saddened by the sight of so much good fish going for fish meal and the association agreed to lower the minimum prices set for small fish to take account of the processors' view. They agreed to sell grades three and four together as grade four while in return the buyers agreed to increase the minimum price from 53p to 60p per stone.

Pushed too far

As if Shetland did not have enough to worry about, with uncertainty over the Common Market, there was also concern because of the constant expansion of territorial limits by other countries in the North Atlantic and the implications for these islands if British distant water trawlers were forced to fish around Shetland.

A special meeting of the executive committee of the SFA was called on 2 November 1974 to discuss the implications of Norway's decision to extend its fisheries limits in the northern area to 50 miles as from 1st January, 1975. It was expected that Faroe would do likewise. It was pointed out at the meeting

that Norwegian and Faroese vessels would still be allowed to fish up to 12 miles from Shetland.

On 24th January, 1975, a rally was held in London to consider a proposal that the UK should extend its fishing limits out to 50 miles. Shetland was represented by skippers Josie Simpson and Mackie Polson, Duncan Robertson of LHD Ltd and Geordie Hunter, Shetland branch chairman of the Herring Producers Association. Speakers in favour of the proposal included Hamish Watt MP and Dr Lyon Dean, chairman of the Herring Industry Board. Another problem facing UK fishermen at this time was the vast amount of fish being imported from European countries outwith the EEC.

Frustration on the part of the British fishermen came to a head at the end of March 1975 with a three-day blockade of British ports. In Shetland an Action Committee of 13 men was elected with Josie Simpson as chairman. Local boats stayed in port to demonstrate their support for their colleagues in the blockade; then on Monday 30th March, they fell in line with the recommendations of the action committee based in Aberdeen, of which Jeemie Wiseman, chairman of the executive committee of the SFA, was a member. For most of that week local boats blockaded both the north and south entrances to Lerwick Harbour and only the P & O vessels from Aberdeen were allowed through.

The Action Committee had six main demands:
- A re-negotiation of the EEC fishing policy as far as it affected the UK
- A 50 mile limit exclusively for British vessels
- A ban on the import of frozen fish and shellfish from non-EEC countries
- A six month ban on the import of fresh fish from non-EEC countries during the summer
- A share of a £2 million subsidy for vessels not included in the Government scheme

• An assurance that registered dock labour would not be introduced into ports where fishermen had become accustomed to land their catches themselves

The blockade of ports was lifted when the Government gave an assurance that it would consider the fishermen's demands.

Time for change in SFA

The additional work brought about by the UK's entry to the Common Market put an added burden on the association's secretary Jeemie Pottinger, now well over the normal age for retirement. He had already given the treasurer's part of the job to Lerwick accountant James A. Daniel.

These negotiations also entailed additional work and travel for SFA chairman Jeemie Wiseman. On 17th May, 1975, he informed a meeting of the executive committee that he could no longer give his full attention to the work of the association without a substantial salary to compensate for the fishing time lost through attending meetings. He added that if this was not forthcoming he would have to resign.

Skipper Robbie Williamson then moved that the time had come for the introduction of a new post of general manager and secretary and since Mr Wiseman had indicated his intention to resign, the executive committee should draw up a short list of candidates for submission to a general meeting of fishermen. The members agreed with this suggestion and decided that in the meantime Mr Pottinger should be given an additional payment of £1000 in recognition of his services over 36 years and that Mr Wiseman should get the sum of £100 for expenses in 1974 and a wage of £70 a week while he was chairman.

On 14th June the executive committee met to consider the six applications for the new post. From these a short list of three were selected – Prophet Smith OBE, Henry Stewart and Geordie Hunter. It was agreed that ballot papers should be sent to all fishermen in Shetland.

The votes were counted on 5th July, 1975. Of the 423 papers distributed 340 had been returned of which four were spoilt. The result was a clear win for Mr Hunter with 226 votes, while Mr Stewart won 69 votes and Prophet Smith 41. A few weeks earlier Mr Hunter had been awarded the MBE in the Queen's birthday honours list, for his services to the fishing industry.

On 9th August at a meeting of the SFA's executive committee in the Fishermen's Mission Mr Hunter outlined his dual role as secretary of the SFA while at the same time trying to get the Scottish Fishermen's Organisation onto a sure footing. It was agreed at that meeting that the executive committee of the SFA, together with the Shetland directors of the SFO should act as port committee for the PO with Jeemie Wiseman as chairman.

In October that year Josie Simpson was appointed chairman of the association and Robbie Williamson its vice-chairman. It was agreed that a change should be made in the composition of the executive committee which should now have one representative for every 40 fishermen. On this basis Whalsay would have four representatives and Burra three while Lerwick and Scalloway would have two each and Unst, Yell, Skerries and Northmavine would have one each.

While Mr Pottinger had worked from home,

Geordie Hunter – an important role in the fishing industry ashore after a lifetime at sea.

Mr Hunter found a small room vacant in Albert Building, Lerwick, where he worked until July 1977 when more suitable office accommodation was obtained in Alexandra Buildings at a rent of £250 per annum. The meetings of the association continued to be held in the Fishermen's Mission until early in 1978, when committee meetings were held in the new SFA office, while annual general meetings, etc were held in the Mission. In April 1980 Mr Hunter obtained part-time clerical assistance from Arthur Makins.

This was a time when Shetlanders' fears regarding the Common Market were at their strongest. In the nationwide referendum of June 1975 Shetlanders voted by 3641 votes to 2815 against the UK remaining within the EEC. The main cause for concern on the part of local people was the possible destruction of the local fishing industry. In the UK as a whole only Shetland and the Western Isles showed a majority against Britain's continuing membership of the Common Market.

The campaign for a 50 mile limit around Shetland received a boost in July 1975 when Shetland Islands Council appointed an action group consisting of councillors Alex Morrison, Edward Thomason, John Butler, William Cumming and Tom Stove, their purpose to fight for safeguards for the local fishing industry. This coincided with the appointment of Jack Burgess as the council's development officer.

The council adopted a three-pronged approach to the local fishing industry – a joint working group consisting of councillors and fishermen's representatives to formulate a policy for the future; financial support for more effective marketing and taking part in lobbying for an acceptable settlement within Europe; and financial aid for both the fish catching and processing industries.

It was recognised that the UK Government had failed miserably in agreeing to join the Common Market on the principle of equal access to fishing grounds, hence the council's support for the idea of local preference in the waters around Shetland.

A further approach to the Government for a 50 mile preference zone for boats based in Shetland was turned down, the Prime Minister Harold Wilson adding his own personal comment that: "such a hasty unilateral measure of this kind would not resolve the over-exploitation of fish stocks."

The action group, soon to be known as the SIC's Fisheries Working Group, continued to exert pressure wherever possible. In May 1977 a council-led delegation to Brussels met Finn Gundelach, Roy Jenkins, John Silken and MPs Gavin Strang, Bruce Millan and Hugh Brown. Again the answer from the politicians was that there was no hope of a 50 mile limit for Shetland.

In February 1978, following a meeting between representatives of the fishing and fish processing industries it was agreed that a joint approach by the two sectors and the council was essential if there was to be any hope of a regional policy for Shetland. By this time the council was talking about a Directorate of Fisheries to be set up by the SIC and financed by the council and both sectors of the industry.

A proposal which got a great deal of support in Shetland was that there should be a ban on fishing by vessels over 80 feet long between perpendiculars in certain areas around Shetland.

Depression in the mid 1970s

A marked depression hit both sectors of the industry in 1975 due in part to decreasing demand for fish products in general, because of the high level of imports by UK processors.

In 1974 the average price of fish landed by seine netters was £7.83 per cwt while in 1975 it fell to £6.62. As a result of poor prices at local markets there was a marked increase in the number of boats tripping to Aberdeen and Peterhead. In 1974 landings at those ports by Shetland vessels amounted to 13,898 cwts valued at £124,760, while in 1975 it rose to 44,229 cwts worth £429,395.

A direct result of low prices was a greater concentration on trawling for industrial species. In 1974 seine netters landed 137,000 cwts and trawlers 35,000 cwts. The following year seiners landed 99,000 cwts of fish while the catch by trawlers soared to 85,000 cwts. While some of the latter was white fish most of it consisted of industrial species. This resulted in a shortage of fish for processors in both 1975 and 1976. Some looked to other sources of supply, Iceatlantic importing 110 tonnes of cod from Poland in an attempt to keep its production lines working.

Iceatlantic had begun another period of expansion. In 1975 the firm installed two Torry kilns for smoking herring and mackerel and had upgraded its production line to handle up to 200 crans of herring each day. It also installed a Baader herring grading machine to solve the problem of very mixed supplies of herring being landed at that time. During the ban on herring fishing in the North Sea and West Coast grounds the firm maintained production by importing frozen herring from Canada.

The recession of the mid 1970s did not shake the confidence of local fishermen. In January 1975 the large steel-hulled trawler *Adonis* was launched at Cambeltown for skipper Magnie Stewart and the *Venturous*, a sturdy vessel with a transom stern was launched for another Whalsay crew (skipper Willie Williamson) while the *Langdale* was bought second-hand for skipper Arthur Polson and partners.

In 1976 the 75ft long *Starina* arrived from Richard Dunston's yard at Thorne in Yorkshire for skipper David Anderson and partners of Whalsay. Two smaller vessels which arrived that year were the *Alis Wood* for a Burra/Scalloway crew (Skipper Alfie Jamieson) and the *Janeen* for skipper Bruce Jamieson of Whalsay, while the stern trawler *Avenger* was bought with assistance of the HIDB for skipper Billy Hughes and three partners from Northmavine.

A large number of old vessels were sold outwith Shetland at this time. They included the *Ocean Reaper, Silver Chord, Gratitude, Glorieuse St Therese* and *La Morlaye* and the smaller boats *Planet, Fertile, Day Dawn* and *Ocean Star*.

An unfortunate incident occurred in January 1976 when the 55ft long *Provider* (skipper Bruce Watt) sank in Yell Sound after hitting an unidentified object. Her crew of three were rescued by the *Concord*.

In March 1976 a smart looking boat arrived at Scalloway – the first new boat to join the village's fleet for ten years. She was the 56ft long *Sparkling Star* built for skipper Jeemie Robb and partners as a replacement for the *White Heather III*. Equipped for both trawling and seine netting, she was powered by a 280hp Kelvin engine.

The industry received a boost that year when the Shetland Fishermen's Trust made the sum of £50,000 available from its income derived from the oil industry for loans to fishermen to buy new or second hand boats.

While fishermen were showing their faith in the future of the industry another group in Whalsay demonstrated their support for the island's white fish processing plant when they took shares in the business.

In the meantime a group of fishermen from Burra and Scalloway were considering the possibility of forming a co-operative. West Side Fishermen Ltd started in 1977 selling chandlery in a shop at Blacksness. It later provided a fuel supply with an old road tanker and in 1979 started a fish selling agency with around ten white fish vessels on its books. In May that year its manager John Arthur Simpson was co-opted onto the executive committee of Shetland Fishermen's Association.

While single boat trawling was rapidly displacing the traditional seine net technique, the Burra boats *Sirius* and *Donvale* were making a success of pair trawling for white fish. In 1975 the Grimsby pair trawlers *Shawnee* and *Mohave* had a highly successful season fishing for cod of Muckle Flugga. The Burra pair followed their example and had an excellent season.

After years of lobbying over the threat to Shetland's fishing industry from foreign trawlers using small meshed nets to catch pout and taking a huge by-catch of other species, the UK Government acted unilaterally in declaring an area closed to pout fishing from the Greenwich meridian to 4 degrees W and between 56 degrees N and 60 degrees N. On 5th March, 1977, at a meeting of the SFA's executive committee it was proposed that the box should be extended from 60 degrees N to 61 degrees N and from 1 degree E to 4 degrees W, operational from 1st January to 31st April each year.

The Pout Box. The area within which fishing for Norway Pout is prohibited, as agreed in 1983.

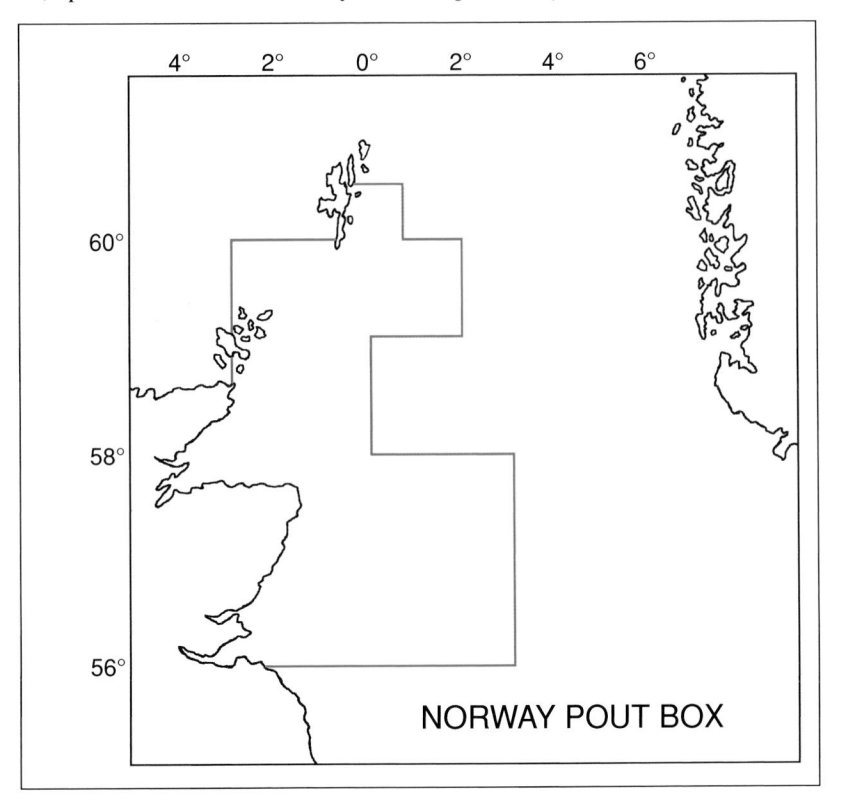

NORWAY POUT BOX

On 12th March, 1977, the local fishery officer attended a special general meeting of the SFA to outline the details of a new order about to be passed by the Government. This would limit the amount of by-catch of a protected species which could be taken in a 16mm industrial trawl to 20 per cent.

Those present were of the opinion that this would do little to save the fishing grounds which were then being "ravished" by industrial trawlers. It was pointed out that the main loophole in the new order was that industrial trawlers could carry a 70mm net as well as a 16mm net and claim that the catch had been taken legally in the former. The meeting agreed that the

Government should be approached to extend the present pout box as proposed at the SFA meeting of 5th March.

Skipper Arthur Polson and crew of the white fish trawler *Langdale*, with the full support of the SFA, succeeded in highlighting the destruction of white fish being carried out around Shetland when, in March 1977, they had their vessel fitted with a 16mm trawl as used by Danish, Norwegian and Faroese industrial trawlers working in the Shetland area.

In a one-hour tow off Unst they caught six tonnes of fish which they separated carefully by species. They selected out one tonne of pout – the rest of the catch consisted of mature and immature haddock and whiting.

Publication of these results in the media made a deep impression on the entire industry and was a major factor in obtaining an extension to the pout box as requested previously by the SFA. It was easier now for the Government to enact this legislation since from 1st January, 1977, Britain had control over the area within 200 miles of its coastline – part of the EEC's territory.

In spite of so many problems Shetland's fishing industry set a new record in 1977 with a catch valued at over £6.8 million, due partly to heavy landings of industrial species which helped to compensate for a scarcity of white fish. There were more problems in 1978 with strict quotas on white fish catches creating problems for both fishermen and processors. In February that year another white fish vessel the 75ft long *Altaire* joined the fleet for skipper John Peter Duncan and partners of Northmavine at a cost of £273,000. They were soon to switch to purse seining with a much larger *Altaire*. During that year the *White Heather*, *Nil Desperandum*, *Heather Belle* and *Bairns Pride* left the islands.

The white fish trawler *Altaire* with a large deck shelter – a step in the evolution of the full shelter deck.

Photo – Robert Johnson

There was keen disappointment in April when Arlanda Fisheries closed its processing plant in Mid Yell, which the company had rescued when its original owners Shetland Seafoods had ceased working there two years earlier. The second closure was attributed to a scarcity of the smaller grades of haddock and whiting and high prices for larger fish. A similar situation occurred a few weeks later when Burra Isle Fisheries closed their factory at Easter Dale.

By June there was an acute shortage of fish which led to severe problems for processors. Some of them were given a respite by importing fish from

Faroe. The scarcity was aggravated by the large number of boats switching to sand-eel fishing. Catches were heavy at times and one vessel, the *Avenger*, sank under the weight of her catch off Fair Isle. Her crew were rescued by another sand-eel trawler the *Constellation*.

The stern trawler *Avenger* in Lerwick Harbour with a large catch of sandeels.

Photo – Martin Smith

There was a keen demand for sand-eels at this time. In addition to the traditional outlet at Bressay, the Norwegian vessel *Sea Crown* bought sand-eels for freezing and Iceatlantic found a market in Norway for its blocks of frozen sand-eels used as mink food. The factory installed its own mechanical unloader on Blacksness Pier to speed up the process of discharging.

During the summer of 1978 it was clear that the UK Government was playing a more decisive role in regulating the fishing industry. The re-negotiation of the Common Fisheries Policy was getting nowhere and it was clear that effort on the grounds around Shetland was intensifying.

Fisheries Minister John Silken made many friends when he announced an extension to the pout box by two degrees between 1st October and 31st March and, more significantly, a cut in the allowable by-catch taken in small mesh nets from 20 per cent to 10 per cent of protected species.

In spite of these concessions the Government still maintained its total opposition to any regional measures to safeguard the local fishing industry. During the summer of 1978 the SFA and the council's Fisheries Working Group combined forces to identify measures which would protect local fish stocks and which would meet with Government approval. It was pointed out that EEC legislation had made provision for regional plans and such a measure was already in force on the west coast of Ireland.

The association agreed to support the SIC if it were to put forward recommendations to prohibit demersal fishing by vessels of all nations over 80ft long between perpendiculars within 50 miles of Shetland and a licensing scheme within that area for a trial period of one year.

These plans came to nothing. On 2nd December the secretary reported to a meeting of the SFA on the outcome of a meeting he had attended at Brussels on 24th and 25th November. A recommendation had been tabled by British ministers for a 12 mile exclusive limit around Shetland and a 50 mile zone of dominant preference. The other EEC ministers had refused even to discuss these proposals.

The year ended with the closure of another white fish plant – that of

Arlanda Fisheries at Lerwick. During the year the value of fish landed at Shetland fell by nearly £1 million compared with 1977 – from £6.8 million to £5.8 million. Of the 1,152,537 cwts landed 667,249 were industrial species.

More new boats joined the fleet in 1979. In March the *Valonia* arrived for skipper Leslie Tait of Trondra. Built at Macduff she was 75.3ft long with a three-quarter length shelter deck. Her deck machinery supplied by the Norwegian firm Karmoy included a large net drum.

In June the 55ft long *Sanlormarho* arrived for skipper Bobby Sutherland of Whalsay while in December the 65ft long *Sonia* arrived for skipper Jeemie Robb of Scalloway to replace the *Sparkling Star* which was sold outwith Shetland. Other boats sold that year were the *Sirius* (sold to an Orkney crew). *Constellation, Janese Watt, Elysian, Ardsheean, Amethyst, Zenith, Janeen* and *Compass Rose*. The old *Research* started her last journey, under tow, to the Scottish Fisheries Museum at Anstruther.

Skipper of the *Sunshine II*, Scott Ward, observes the catch being lifted onboard.

The Shetland Fishing Plan

The main event of 1979 was the publication of a detailed Shetland Fishing Plan. Its author John Goodlad was a member of a prominent fishing family in Burra who had had an interest in the fishing industry since childhood. While a student at Aberdeen University he spent his summer holidays as a crewman on local seine net vessels.

After graduating in 1978 with an MA (Hons) degree in geography he began work on a post-graduate thesis on the history of Shetland's fishing industry for which he was awarded another degree, Master of Literature (M.Litt.). Incorporated in this was a specific project sponsored jointly by Shetland Islands Council and the White Fish Authority, which was published separately as the Shetland Fishing Plan.

After recording the background to the industry, its resource base and its context within European fisheries and its importance to the local economy, the report recommended a fisheries management scheme with two main objectives: the conservation of fish stocks in order to provide a more rational exploitation pattern and a regional preference for the Shetland fishing industry. It called for a Shetland fisheries management scheme within a huge sea area from 59 degrees N to 62 degrees N and covering most of the area from 4 degrees W to the EEC/Norway median line in the east. Within this "box" there would be a preference for Shetland vessels.

While every Shetland vessel would receive a licence automatically to fish within this area, the report recommended that vessels which had traditionally fished there should also receive licences.

The plan was presented to Shetland Islands Council in September 1979 and was discussed by the executive committee of the SFA on 5th October. It was given a good reception although the skippers of six purse seiners later wrote to the secretary expressing their fears that the plan did not give adequate

John Goodlad.

protection to the pelagic sector. It was finally accepted by both the council and the SFA.

Mr Goodlad was to retain an advisory position with the council when in 1980 he was appointed to the newly created post of Fisheries Development Officer within the council's development department.

In December 1979 skipper Josie Simpson resigned after serving as SFA chairman for a full three year term. He was succeeded by skipper Bert Laurenson with Magnie Stewart as vice-chairman.

At a meeting of the executive committee on 4th April, 1980, Mr Simpson was presented with an inscribed table lighter in recognition of his services during a particularly eventful term of office which had seen quotas introduced, EEC regulations brought into force and lengthy negotiations in Europe and within the UK. Mr Simpson had been at the forefront of all these efforts, giving a great deal of time and knowledge for the good of the association.

A break with the traditional boat design was apparent in 1980 with the arrival of five steel-hulled vessels built in Norway. They were the 78ft long *Madalia* for skipper Alistair Thomason of Yell and an identical vessel, the *Maverick*, for skipper Duncan Cumming of Burra; and three 45ft long inshore vessels, the *Krisona* (Richard Gray), *Aquarius* (Jim Smith) and *Day Dawn* (Robbie Watt).

The three small boats incorporated many features previously restricted to much larger vessels. Wheelhouse and crew's quarters were for'ard leaving the entire after deck clear for trawling, with winch, net drum and gallows aft.

There was considerable excitement in Foula that year when Kenneth and David Gear acquired the small stern trawler *Vol au Vent*, the biggest vessel ever owned by Foula people. Another addition to the Whalsay fleet in September was the 56ft long *Flourish* for skipper Joe Kay.

There was better news for the processing sector when the plant at Easterdale, Burra, having been bought by the SIC, was leased to L. Williamson (Shetland) Ltd and the factory at Northmavine was reopened to produce boil in the bag, vacuum-packed pet food.

It was a year of dramatic incidents, fortunately without loss of life. In January the *Brighter Morn* hit rocks near the Ord of Bressay and became a total loss, her crew being rescued from their liferaft by Lerwick lifeboat. She was replaced by the 57ft long *Aspire*. In September the *Maverick*, only three months old, sank after grounding near Fair Isle.

A major problem arose in 1980 when a high proportion of grade three whiting on local markets led to large quantities of fish remaining unsold. This was happening all round the Scottish coast and in mid-February The Scottish Fishermen's Organisation reached a stage where it could no longer provide compensation for withdrawn fish.

The situation was again being aggravated by the high volume of imports, as was pointed out at a protest meeting attended by 700 fishermen at Peterhead. It was agreed that the Government should be given one month to find a solution to the problem.

The Government responded by making £14 million available to help the industry although there was no clear idea as to how it should be spent. Two suggestions mooted locally were a price support scheme and a subsidy to reduce the price of fuel. Shetland Islands Council offered a subsidy to all processors to encourage them to buy more fish, offering £2 per box for all fish bought above their normal weekly purchases.

Shetland Fishermen's Association decided to take control of the local situation with its own minimum price structure, a modified price support arrangement coupled to a flexible quota system and compensation for withdrawn fish, funded by levies on the boxes that were sold. This scheme came into operation during October and worked extremely well. It remained in force until the end of the year when the SFO accepted EEC withdrawal prices. However the local quota system remained in place for some time in an attempt to reduce the need for compensation payments.

The local industry received a severe blow with the sudden death of association secretary Geordie Hunter at Brussels on 18th November, 1980. He had attended a meeting aimed at settling outstanding issues regarding the Common Fisheries Policy. It had been a useful meeting and the Shetland delegation was satisfied with the progress made. His death came only a few weeks after that of councillor Alex Morrison, a man who, like Geordie, had spent a lifetime promoting Shetland's fishing industry.

Again the SFA had to go through the process of seeking nominations for the post of secretary and general manager of Shetland Fishermen's Association with ballot papers sent to all fishermen. There were five candidates – George Bannerman, Alan Coghill, Jim Henry, John Goodlad and Magnie Stewart. The outcome was a clear win for John Goodlad with 253 votes out of the 371 valid papers returned.

Mr Goodlad had to give three months notice to his employers, Shetland Islands Council, and took up his new post in February 1981. His successor as fisheries development officer was Jim Henry. Arthur Makins who had been assistant to Mr Hunter acted as secretary until Mr Goodlad was free to take up his new appointment.

He started work in the middle of another serious dispute, brought about because of low demand and poor prices. The Peterhead fishermen had decided to go on strike and they found backing from most areas, including Shetland. Shetland fishermen took the unusual step of holding a general meeting on a Sunday (22nd February) when they agreed to go back to sea.

Towards a settlement

The first meeting of the SFA's executive committee with John Goodlad as secretary was held on 23rd May, 1981, when the Shetland Fishing Plan was at the top of the agenda.

Mr Goodlad had to defend the plan from an onslaught by councillor Henry Stewart who suggested that the plan should be abandoned in favour of an exclusive 12 mile limit around Orkney and Shetland.

Mr Goodlad pointed out that the final plan, if accepted, would be of much greater benefit to the Shetland fishing industry than a 12 mile limit by itself. He reminded Mr Stewart that to advocate a 12 mile limit would antagonise the entire British fishing industry, making it certain that national organisations like the Scottish Fishermen's Federation would not accept a Common Fisheries Policy which incorporated this measure. Moreover the sudden abandonment of the plan after two years of negotiation would result in Shetland losing credibility with EEC officials and the UK Government.

The committee agreed to back the Shetland fishing plan with the proviso that if it should be turned down all possibilities, including a 12 mile limit, would be explored.

Little progress was made at Brussels during 1982. There was a suspicion that France and Denmark did not want a settlement, preferring to play for time and wait until the concession which extended the UK rights to a 12 mile limit expired. French and Dutch delegates were complaining about the proposed "Shetland Box" and there was concern on the part of British trawler owners that some of their vessels would be excluded.

In July a steering group was formed to consider the advantages of forming a Shetland Fish Producers' Organisation. This was influenced to a great extent by the success of the local price scheme in the autumn of 1980 which contrasted markedly with the failure of the SFO to control markets that year. It was pointed out that a 12 month notice of resignation was required by the SFO.

Several additions were made to the local fleet in 1981. In March the *Sunbeam* arrived for skipper John Garriock and partners, built by Campbeltown Shipyard at a cost of £600,000. In April the inshore boat *Steadfast* arrived from Norway for the Johnson family of Vidlin. Other arrivals that year were the big seiner/trawler *Evening Star* for skipper Davie Smith of Scalloway, the 55ft long *Horizon* for the Hughson family of Skerries and the steel-hulled *Ardent* built in Sweden for skipper Kenneth Pottinger of Hamnavoe. The old *Evening Star* was sold to a Burra partnership led by skipper Theo Fullerton.

There were losses too. On Sunday 3rd May the *Day Dawn* sank off Helliness while on her way to Lerwick with a load of sand-eels. Her crew were rescued. Less than a month later the *Valonia* sank off Stronsay while heading for Fraserburgh to discharge her catch of sand-eels. Her crew were rescued from their liferaft by the Whalsay boat *Langdale*.

The *Valonia* was replaced by a new boat the *Gratitude*, which unfortunately was lost on rocks near Mousa a year later. It was another severe blow for a promising young skipper Leslie Tait who later had a highly successful career with the seiner/trawler *Harmony*.

Another dispute between fishermen and fish merchants arose early in 1982 when it was realised that buyers were getting far more than six stones of fish in a "six stone" box and the SFA decided to raise the nominal weight to 6½ stones. After a lot of wrangling the issue was settled when fishermen agreed

A delegation representing Orkney and Shetland attending a Fisheries Council in Luxembourg in 1981. Back row (from left): Jackie Hughson (SFA); Sandy Cluness (SIC); John Goodlad (SIC); Duncan Robertson (SFA/LHD); Chris Zawadski (OIC). Front row (from left): Alan Coghill (OIC); Geordie Hunter (SFA); Henry Stewart (SIC); and Lady Gillian Whelter (SIC public relations consultant).

to make sure that no more than six stones of fish were put in the boxes. Jeemsie Henry was employed to weigh a selection of boxes to make sure that this weight was adhered to. He was assisted by retired skipper and past SFA chairman Jeemsie Ward.

A further setback for the association came in December 1982 when the Scottish Fishermen's Federation rejected the principle of fisheries management based on regional or local preference and control. At a meeting of the executive committee on 22nd December it was agreed that the association should remain within the Federation to try and amend its policy on this matter. If no progress was made, however, the SFA would consider leaving the Federation.

This was also the year when the White Fish Authority and Herring Industry Board were wound up, being merged into a new Sea Fish Industry Authority.

Political issues were overshadowed in January 1983 when two Lerwick men, Ellis Sales (45) and Bruce Mair (18) were lost overboard from the *Avrella* four miles east of the Bard. It was their first trip after purchasing the vessel along with skipper Delano Jennings and another two men.

Settlement at last

After many years of negotiation agreement on a revised Common Fishery Policy was eventually reached in Brussels on Tuesday 25th January, 1983. It had been a long and tedious debate with many meetings in Brussels at which association representatives had faithfully lobbied during the years.

While no group of European fishermen had received all that they had been asking for, there was a general relief that a compromise had been reached and that a policy was in place. A deal had been signed which would last for twenty years with a review at the end of ten years. It provided for a retention throughout the twenty year period of the six and 12 mile limits for all member states including the UK. It agreed a permanent shareout of quotas to member states. The UK obtained some particularly generous quotas. For example it obtained 78% of North Sea haddock and 58% of western mackerel. This method of sharing out quotas became known as the principle of relative stability. The controversial Norway pout box was at long last accepted as a European measure instead of simply a unilateral UK restriction. A variety of technical conservation measures (covering issues such as minimum mesh sizes and minimum landing sizes) was also agreed as was a control regulation which, for the first time, took steps to ensure that all aspects of fisheries were properly policed throughout the Common Market.

Finally, agreement was finally reached on the Shetland Box Licensing Scheme. Within a wide area around Orkney and Shetland, large demersal fishing vessels of more than 26 metres in length would in future require a special licence before they could operate there. Up to 128 of these vessels were to be allowed to fish at any one time. The UK would have 62 licences, France 52, Germany 12 and Belgium 2. The association criticised the licensing scheme on the grounds that too many licences had been issued in the first place and than no licensing system had been introduced for vessels of less than 26 metres. In view of the importance which the association had placed on securing a regional licensing scheme around Shetland, the association refused to back the Scottish Fishermen's Federation in publicly supporting the UK Government in signing up for the CFP deal. Despite this, however, the association was able to take some considerable satisfaction in the fact that, had it not been for its intensive lobbying over the previous four years, it was unlikely that the Shetland Box would ever have featured at all as part of the revised Common Fisheries Policy.

At long last a settlement had been reached after so many years of arguing. The date of special significance to the Scottish delegation since it was Burns night. Shetlanders at the meeting were aware that it was also the night of Lerwick's Up-Helly-A'. Both delegations had a double reason for the celebrations.

The Shetland Box. The area within which fishing by larger vessels is restricted, as agreed in 1983.

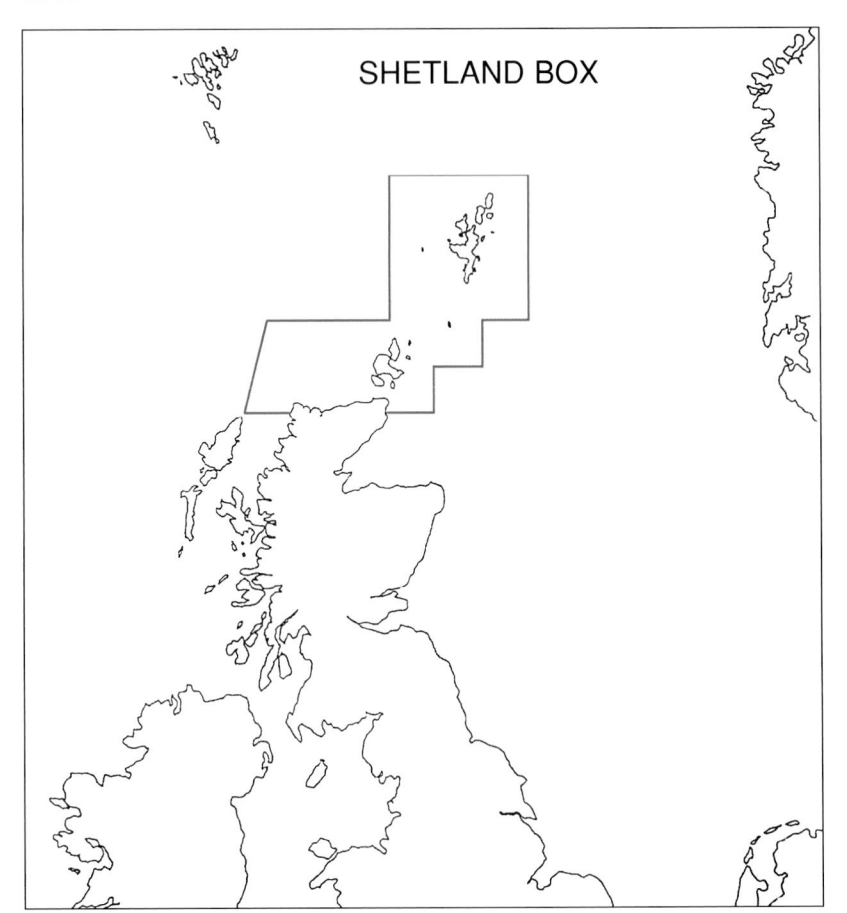

SHETLAND BOX

CHAPTER SEVEN

A decade of expansion

Agreement on a common fisheries policy did not end the long debate over the protection of fish stocks around Shetland. At a meeting of the executive committee of the SFA on 26th February, 1983, members stressed their continuing support for a regional management scheme. While still at odds with the Scottish Fishermen's Federation over this issue, members decided to remain within that body, even though two constituent associations had resigned. It was also agreed to maintain the association's close working relationship with Shetland Islands Council on fisheries management issues through the fisheries working group.

The association welcomed the setting up of the Alex Morrison and George L. Hunter Memorial Trust with a target fund of £20,000 and decided to donate £3000 to the trust. One of its first moves was to provide two trophies, to be awarded annually to the vessels achieving the highest gross earnings for fish landed in Shetland – the George L. Hunter Memorial Trophy for boats over 60ft long and the Alex Morrison Trophy for those under 60ft long. First winners, for catches in 1983, were the *Sunbeam* (John Garriock) and the *Flourish* (Joe Kay), for earnings of £332,773 and £144,248 respectively.

It wasn't long before the wide ranging nature of EEC legislation became apparent. On 23rd April, 1983, the executive committee of the SFA considered a draft regulation produced by the EEC Working Group on the "Harmonisation of the social and working conditions of fishermen." The executive committee realised that the fishing industry had "a major public relations task" in pointing out "the impracticability and irrelevance of these proposals to the inshore sector of the industry."

Another cause for concern was "control and enforcement", especially the over-zealous attitude of the UK Government, which contrasted markedly with the apparent lack of enforcement by other member states.

While failure to fix herring quotas for 1983 was still holding up agreement on other quotas, several conservation measures were approved at the October Fisheries Council. Clarification was obtained with regard to the operation of the Shetland Box. A literal interpretation of the rules required boats to report to the EEC Commission each time they entered or left a port within that area. The association pointed out that this would have serious implications for vessels fishing out of local ports on a daily basis. It was agreed that weekly reporting would be adequate for locally based vessels.

There was a deferment of the proposed increase in mesh sizes in seine nets and trawls, which would also give time for a study into the impact such an increase would have on boats fishing for whiting.

The UK Government acted quickly to exert control over its part of Common Market waters with a licensing scheme covering "pressure stocks" – those species where the UK allocation was likely to be taken up or where catching potential exceeded the allocation. The fisheries involved were west coast mackerel and North Sea herring, cod, haddock and whiting. All vessels over 10m long had to be licensed and a licence for a boat under 10m long could not be transferred to a bigger one.

The SFA had advocated a national licensing authority to control and monitor any licensing arrangements. It was argued that the absence of such an authority would result in licences accruing a monetary value, while the lack of such a body would make the implementation of the concept of regional preference in the allocation of licences more difficult.

Ironically the SFA supported a proposal in the Inshore Fishing (Scotland) Bill that the age-old ban on trawling within the three-mile limit should be removed. Having long been regarded as a form of protection for small boats, it was now a major deterrent to the activities of small vessels fishing for sand-eels.

However, it was agreed that a submission should be made to the Government, calling for a ban on pair trawling and beam trawling within six miles of Shetland and a ban on all types of demersal fishing by vessels over 80 feet registered length within six miles of the shore. When the Inshore Fishing (Scotland) Bill was being debated on 23rd October, 1985, fishermen from Orkney and Shetland, along with representatives of the two islands councils, mounted a strong lobby of MPs without success.

The SFA welcomed the findings of the Montgomery Committee of Inquiry into the functions and powers of island authorities in Scotland, particularly the recommendation that the Secretary of State should recognise the need for some element of local control in fisheries management.

An old problem resurfaced when the EEC Fisheries Council of 10th September, 1984, decided to increase the permitted by-catch of protected species in the fishery for Norway pout from 10 per cent to 18 per cent. The UK ministerial team agreed to a compromise proposal that the by-catch could be increased to 18 per cent, of which no more than 8 per cent could be of white fish species other than whiting. It was also agreed that this new regulation should be a temporary one – from 1st October, 1984, to 31st May, 1985, during which time the Commission would monitor the situation very closely.

This compromise led to a furious reaction from the Scottish and Shetland delegations, who had travelled to Brussels to lobby the meeting of the Fisheries Council. The UK Fisheries Ministers were literally left standing alone when they reported the outcome of the meeting, as the UK fishing industry delegations walked out. Among the Shetland delegation were councillors Willie Cumming and Henry Stewart, along with SFA secretary John Goodlad.

The association agreed that the time had come for another demonstration of the destruction caused by pout fishing. The Whalsay boat *Aquila* was equipped with an industrial trawl with a mesh of 16mm and in March 1985 she carried out a series of hauls about 30 miles east of Bressay. On every occasion there was a huge by-catch of protected species – as high as 80 per cent with an average of 26.25 per cent. Press reporters were on board to record the findings and a video was made of each haul. The subsequent publicity in local

The *Aquila*'s catch, which proved conclusively the damage being done to the fish stocks by industrial trawlers. In the picture are John Sales and John Arthur Poleson.

Photo – Malcolm Younger

and national newspapers played a big part in having the permitted by-catch reduced back to 10 per cent.

In the meantime local fishermen were learning how to satisfy further regulations emanating from Brussels as from 1st April, 1985, they had to fill in log books and landing declarations for each trip.

Shetland's own PO

While negotiations to reform the Common Fisheries Policy were still going on Shetland fishermen had taken steps to secure a greater degree of control over their own affairs. They had agreed to form a Shetland Fish Producers Organisation as a complement to the long established Shetland Fishermen's Association. Producer organisations had been set up in the UK following Britain's entry into the Common Market. Although they had been founder members of the Scottish Fishermen's Organisation (SFO) the Shetland fishermen began to realise that their interests would be served better by having their own Fish Producers Organisation.

The first meeting of the Shetland PO was held on 11th September, 1982, when a draft constitution was approved. It was decided that there should be 12 elected directors – eight from the white fish sector and four representing the pelagic sector. It was also agreed that the funds of the two groups should be kept separate.

There were four nominations from the pelagic sector, Bruce Anderson (*Aquila*), Josie Simpson (*Azalea*), Robbie Williamson (*Research*) and Lowrie Irvine (*Antares*), thus avoiding the need for an election. There were 14 nominations for the eight white fish directorships. Those receiving most votes were David Anderson (*Starina*), Johnnie Anderson (*Vagrant*), Peter Goodlad (*Dewy Rose*), Ewen Mowat (*Pescoso*), Jeemie Robb (*Sonia*), Johnnie Sales (*Welfare*), Alistair Sandison (*Korona*) and Russell Smith (*Aspire*).

At a subsequent meeting Josie Simpson was appointed chairman and Jeemie Robb vice-chairman. It was agreed that representatives of LHD Ltd and West Side Fishermen Ltd should be co-opted as directors. John Goodlad was appointed chief executive and Brian Isbister was appointed to the new post of administrative assistant.

One of the main functions of the PO was to handle compensation fund payments from the EEC for fish that failed to find a buyer. The PO also had powers to regulate landings so that withdrawals were kept within bounds. Landings were heavy in the early part of 1983 and withdrawals were as high as 10 per cent in the case of haddock so the PO decided to operate a flexible weekly quota.

The PO also had powers to enforce whatever regulations were necessary, with fines for member vessels which exceeded their weekly quota or sold fish privately.

After a successful first year when withdrawals were kept to an extremely low level, the PO was entrusted with its own sectoral quota for haddock with 6500 tonnes to allocate among its 70 member vessels. Eventually it was given its own sectoral quota for all other species after operating within national quotas for a few years.

Within a fairly short period the Shetland PO had progressed from operating the withdrawal price scheme to managing its own fish quotas. This was to become an extremely important role for the PO in later years.

The Shetland PO continued to rise in importance to become a major force in the local fishing industry. However its management responsibility never in any way threatened the political role of Shetland Fishermen's Association, which remained the organisation through which the fishermen of Shetland sought to make their views known on a variety of issues at local, national and European levels. Indeed both have effectively complemented each other and have always operated from the same office and employed the same staff.

The herring stocks recover

During the ban on fishing for herring Shetland's pelagic fleet underwent a remarkable transformation, influenced in part by the much longer periods spent at sea while searching for mackerel. Late in 1977 the *Azalea* was taken to a shipyard in Holland where she was cut in two and had a new section complete with RSW tanks inserted amidships. The *Serene* and *Wavecrest* underwent similar treatment.

Other skippers decided to replace their old vessels with new ones incorporating the latest improvements. In December 1978 a new *Antares*, 107 feet long, was built in Norway for Lowrie Irvine and Partners. In July 1979 the *Charisma* joined the fleet, built at Flekkefjord in Norway for the previous unheard of price of £1.25m. The next arrival, in November that year, was the *Altaire* for John Peter Duncan and partners as a replacement for the white fish vessel named *Altaire*. The new vessel was 120 feet long and carried her catch in six RSW tanks.

In January 1980 Josie Simpson regained the length record with a new *Azalea* 130 feet long. He held that record until October that year when the 133ft long *Research* was built for Willie Williamson and partners, replacing the two smaller boats – the purse seiner *Unity* and the white fish trawler *Venturous* which had worked together as partners.

The purse seiner *Research* which held the length record in 1980.

There was a delay until June 1985 when the next *Antares* arrived. She had been built in Norway in 1980 as the Banff-registered *Radiant Star*. The former

Antares became the *Serene* and the previous *Serene* was sold to a crew in Fraserburgh.

A major problem for the pelagic sector was the long tie-up between the end of the winter fishery for mackerel off south-west England and the start of the autumn fishery off north-west Scotland. Some boats went trawling for white fish during the winter, while in 1980 the *Wavecrest* fished with gillnets for several weeks landing 741cwts of ling and cod. The *Antares* and *Charisma* spent some time fishing for horse mackerel, while the *Azalea* fished for blue whiting, these catches being landed at the Bressay fish meal factory.

In 1982 the White Fish Authority carried out extensive experiments in the Iceatlantic factory at Scalloway, having installed processing equipment which proved that blue whiting, found west of Shetland from March to May each year, could be processed into a variety of low-priced food products.

The first sign of recovery in the herring stocks came in August 1981, when the EEC Commission approved the reopening of the Minch fishery with a total allowable catch of 65,000 tonnes, of which 37,000 tonnes were awarded to UK vessels. The result was a mad scramble by the fleets taking part to make sure that they got their share of the total catch. Home markets were swamped with herring and large quantities went for fish meal.

Late in 1982 the EEC allocated a TAC of 20,000 tonnes of herring from the southern North Sea. When British vessels had taken a mere 700 tonnes the fishery was closed when it was realised that Denmark, allocated 1000 tonnes had taken 11,500 tonnes while there was no record of what the French fleet had caught.

Skipper Davie Hutchison of the Whalsay purse seiner m.v. *Charisma*.

Photo – Deborah Lamb

The chaos that marked this fishery made it clear to fisheries ministers at Brussels that they had to do a lot of homework to perfect their system for allocating and enforcing national quotas.

In 1983 there was a partial reopening of the North Sea fishery with 4656 tonnes brought to Lerwick worth £643,882, while in 1984 the catch rose to 17,031 tonnes valued at £2,212,000. It was a season which highlighted the imbalance in the fishery with very few jobs created ashore. None of the curing firms had survived the seven years ban on herring fishing and the main outlet onshore was Iceatlantic at Scalloway, which bought several hundred tonnes for freezing, kippering and marinating.

The main outlet that year was the fleet of 17 East European klondykers which anchored in Lerwick harbour, having delayed their arrival while their agents argued with the Shetland PO over the price to be paid, claiming that the EEC minimum price of £135 per tonne was too high. The klondykers realised that they were practically the only outlet and could dictate the price which was as low as £107 per tonne that year.

It was clear that a fresh look at marketing was required if Shetland was to take full advantage of a rejuvenated herring fishery. It was obvious to many people that the answer lay in a large new processing plant to freeze herring whole and filleted and provide a large number of jobs locally. While the herring stocks had recovered, the ban on fishing had produced another benefit in the form of a winter mackerel fishery which Shetland had never had before.

An unexpected problem arose with the Department of Agriculture and Fisheries, since Lerwick had lost its status as a landing port for herring and mackerel. It was now a klondyking port and vessels fishing for a home market should in theory have to go to Fraserburgh or Peterhead where local outlets had survived.

A processing plant of the type envisaged for Lerwick was one of the main recommendations in a report on the future of Shetland's fishing industry prepared by Dr Alistair Goodlad for Shetland Islands Council and published in May 1984. The report also called for improvements throughout the fish catching sector as well as in harbour facilities. It also recommended the formation of a joint marketing company to obtain better prices for the end product.

Lerwick Harbour Trust was quick to respond to the proposal for a pelagic processing plant and a site was earmarked initially at Holmsgarth on land reclaimed as part of the final phase of development in a scheme which had produced the P & O terminal and the Morrison Dock. By the end of 1985 plans had been drawn up and an operating company, Shetland Pelagic Processing (Lerwick) Ltd, had been formed with two shareholders, the Shetland PO and Lerwick Harbour Trust. The proposed factory would handle around 20,000 tonnes of herring and mackerel each year. It would cost around £7 million and would provide around 100 permanent jobs.

The *Adenia* in a drydock at Hull, cut in two and waiting for a new section to be inserted amidships.

Photo – Walter Fussey & Sons

The proposed investment by the Shetland PO in a new plant was a decision of enormous importance for the fishermen of Shetland. Through their producer organisation the fishermen of Shetland were, for the first time, prepared to become the major players in Shetland's fish processing industry. This was a trend which would continue through other investments in fish processing.

By 1985 the recovery of the herring stocks was well under way and Lerwick had its biggest catch for 50 years with 27,686 tonnes worth more than £3 million. This accounted for over 40 per cent of the UK national quota.

Converted into old units the season's catch was the equivalent of 184,573 crans, caught by a British fleet of 30 purse seiners. In 1935, when the catch was over 200,000 crans, the fleet had numbered 304 drifters at its height. The "shoreworkers" had numbered 1850 of whom 1300 were gutters, filling 246,450 barrels for export. In 1985 the people who handled the catch again numbered around 2000 – practically all of them on klondykers anchored in Lerwick Harbour, where the fleet reached a peak of 34 vessels.

The local pelagic fleet continued to expand. In December 1985 the 19 year old Norwegian purse seiner *Klaring* was bought by Morris Duncan of Ollaberry and partners. She was later renamed *Advance*. 1986 saw the departure

The crew of the *Azalea*, back row, from left: John J. Shearer, Stewart Anderson, Magnus Hutchison, John A Shearer, Josie Simpson and Wilbert Jamieson. Front row, from left: Bobby Sandison, Tammy Simpson, Robbie Irvine and Magnie Reid.

of Shetland's first purpose-built purse seiner, the *Wavecrest*, to start a new career in Macduff. It also saw the return of the *Antares* from Norway, where she had been lengthened to make her 188 feet long – the largest vessel in the islands.

In October 1986 the *Adenia* resumed fishing after having a large section inserted amidships, giving a new lease of life to a vessel which had been built in France in 1975. Another elderly Norwegian purse seiner the *Fiskebas* joined the fleet, having been purchased by John W. Stewart and partners, using the pelagic licence transferred from the *Aquila*, which was now concentrating on white fish.

In June 1987 the 180ft long *King's Cross* became the fourth *Research*, her predecessor having been sold to a consortium in North East Scotland. A month later a new *Altaire* arrived from Norway where she had been built at a cost of £5 million. With a length of 200 feet she was the largest fishing vessel then in Shetland and, combining trawling and purse seining capabilities, she was the first of a new generation of pelagic vessels.

In October 1987 the *Azalea* returned from Denmark where she had been cut in two having a huge 61½ft long section inserted amidships and an extra section at the stern. With a length of 201 feet she was now the longest pelagic vessel in the UK.

Even she was dwarfed by the 227ft long *Shetland Challenger* (LK143), built for the North Atlantic Fishing Company (Shetland) Ltd – a factory trawler designed for operating in Arctic waters and having the ability to process her entire catch on board. She was owned by a consortium which included one Shetlander, Morris Duncan, the remaining shareholders being Norwegian. Although she was registered in the UK this was merely a flag of convenience to obtain additional fishing rights in UK waters. She was not allowed to have membership of the Shetland PO or the Shetland Fishermen's Association. While her connection with Shetland was very brief it allowed several Shetland men and women to experience fishing for shrimps and other species in the Arctic.

The distant water factory trawler *Shetland Challenger*, the biggest vessel to have the registration letters LK.

Photo – Robert Johnson

It was purely by coincidence that John Peter Duncan and partners had the *Altaire* lengthened in Norway to 240 feet making her the largest fishing vessel in the UK. With three extra tanks inserted amidships she now had the capacity to carry 2000 tonnes of fish. Her crew had had several big catches of blue whiting and the extra tanks made her more efficient on long distance trips. The next fishery which they were anxious to try was one for argentines, found in deep water to the north-west of Britain.

The white fish fleet expands

The pressure stock restrictive licensing scheme introduced by the UK Government had been intended to limit the capacity of the UK fishing fleet. Before a partnership could obtain approval for having a new vessel built it had to decommission an older one. Scrapping grants were introduced as an incentive to do so.

Surprisingly there was no limit set on the size of the replacement vessel in the over 40 feet group. It was only in May 1987 that Fisheries Minister John Gummer announced an important change in the rules by stipulating that it was no longer permissible to transfer a pressure stock licence from a vessel under 80 feet to one over 80 feet.

In the years before this rule was introduced scores of large modern vessels had replaced smaller vessels in fishing ports throughout the UK. Shetland fishermen had an advantage over their counterparts in most parts of the country, thanks to grants and loans offered by Shetland Islands Council, in addition to funding available in most cases by the HIDB, the Sea Fish Authority and the EEC. There was also a low interest fund set up by the Shetland Fishermen's Trust to assist new partnerships.

In 1982 the 50ft long *Andromeda* was built for Robbie Watt and partners of Lerwick as a replacement for the *Day Dawn*. In 1983 Leslie Tait and partners acquired the *Hazelmore* which they renamed *Harmony*, while the 34ft long shellfish boat *Brilliant* was acquired by Michael Watt of Scalloway and given the unique number LK1.

In 1984 the 60ft long white fish vessel *Osprey* was built at St Monans for skipper Raymie Smith and Jeemie Williamson to replace the old MFV *Jessie*

Sinclair, which was soon to be scrapped, while the 67ft long *Ariane* was built for skipper Larry Williamson and partners of Burra. Another addition to the Burra fleet that year was the *Freedom IV* bought by Ralph Pottinger and partners and renamed *Sunrise*. An addition to the Whalsay fleet that year was the 42ft long *Harvest Home*, bought by Peter Williamson.

An unusual acquisition in 1984 was the Aberdeen trawler *Grampian Heather*, bought by Russell Smith and partners and renamed *Achieve C.S.* Before resuming fishing she was totally enclosed by a shelter deck – a major operation carried out by HNP Engineers of Lerwick.

The owners of the *Achieve*: Billy Hughson, Ronnie Couper, Ian Walterson, Russell Smith and Lyndon Mouat.

Inevitably many old vessels were withdrawn from service at this time, others were lost and some were damaged beyond repair. In April 1983 the *Victory* sank off Vaila while on her way to Scalloway with a catch of sandeels when her for'ard bulkhead gave way. She had been bought from her previous owners in Whalsay by Stephen Gray from Skeld.

In October 1983 the old Burra boat *Replenish* was scrapped after being damaged by fire. She had been bought by Russell Smith and Robert Couper as a pair trawling partner for their current vessel *Aspire*. A few weeks later the *Good Tidings* was damaged by fire. She was sold later to a partnership in Cleethorpes.

In May 1984 skipper Tommy Fullerton retired and his vessel the *Sceptre* was sold to a crew from Wick, while the *Sanlormarho* went to Lossiemouth. Later that year the *Welfare* (ex-*John West*) left Lerwick to start a new career in Malta; and the *Unity*, owned by Morris Duncan, sank off the Ramna Stacks, her crew being rescued by the *Aspire*.

About this time there was news that the former Skerries boat *St Clair*, later renamed *Valorous* and used in salvage work on the wreck of the *SS Oceanic* near Foula, had been arrested at Tripoli when she was found to be carrying 10 tonnes of drugs.

An important addition to the Burra fleet in 1985 was the 80ft long *Be Ready*, built at Campbeltown for Theo Fullerton and partners of Hamnavoe at a cost of £700,000, to replace the smaller wooden vessel *Opportune* which was sold to John Anderson and partners. She was followed by the *Adonis*, an 85ft long vessel built at Campbeltown for skipper Duncan Cumming and partners at a cost of £800,000. Her massive hold had a capacity for 2000

The *Be Ready* hauling her net.

boxes. At that time she was the biggest white fish vessel ever built for Shetland owners. The previous *Adonis* was sold to a company in Aberdeen.

A week after the *Adonis* arrived the 60ft long wooden vessel *Contest* arrived at Whalsay for Johnnie Anderson and partners as a replacement for the *Vagrant*. Then in July another 80ft Campbeltown boat the *Donvale II* arrived at Burra for Jimmy Fullerton and partners. The older *Donvale* went to Fraserburgh.

Lerwick skipper Johnnie Sales on board m.v. *Guiding Light*.

Photo – Deborah Lamb

Boats sold outwith Shetland in 1985 included the *Concord* to Northern Ireland, and the *Sunshine II* to Cairnbulg. The *Scotch Queen*, which had been in Shetland since 1952, and the *Sunrise* (ex-*Sunbeam*) were sold to become diving tenders and the *Avrella* started a new career in Glasgow.

The first arrival in 1986 was the 70ft long wooden vessel *Trident* for Jeemie Robb and partners of Scalloway, built by Jones of Buckie. Mr Robb's previous vessel *Sonia* had been sold to Jeemie Anderson who had previously owned the *Avrella*. Next arrival was the 56ft long *Fertile* bought second hand by John David Anderson of Skerries. Next came the 76ft steel-hulled *Prevail*, built at St Monans for Robert Irvine and partners of Whalsay.

The most unusual arrival that year was the *Guiding Light* for Johnnie Sales and partners of Lerwick. Her hull was built by the Yorkshire Dry Dock Company and after the casing, wheelhouse and shelterdeck were added she was towed north to Fraserburgh for completion by J. & G. Forbes of Sandhaven. In March that year an older trawler the *Kingsdale*, built at Aberdeen in 1973, arrived at Scalloway for a group of local men led by Arthur Johnson, who at 24 was the youngest skipper in the local fleet. A smaller addition to the shellfish fleet was the *Craignair* bought by Leslie Gray of Burravoe, Yell.

There was a minor sensation in Shetland that summer when skipper Russell Smith and partners purchased the 130ft long stern trawler *Arctic Reiver* from Boyd Line and renamed her *Vega*. Although she had been laid up for some time, due to her previous poor performance, she proved to he highly successful under her new owners. Only a few weeks after her transfer to Shetland she made headline news by landing a catch of squid at Lochinver to earn £86,000. Skipper Smith's previous vessel *Achieve* was sold to Alex Hutchison and partners of Whalsay to replace the *Concord* which had been sold to a partnership in Ireland.

There were more additions to the Shetland fleet in 1986. John Anderson and partners had the *Still Waters* built at Buckie to replace the *Opportune*,

The 130ft long *Vega*, a success story under a Shetland crew.

Photo – Robert Johnson

Sunbeam skipper John Garriock, and crew, celebrate winning the George L. Hunter Memorial Trophy in 1995. Back row, from left: Willie Abernethy, Bobby Sandison, Martin Hay, Norman Fraser, Jake Garrick, Arthur Johnson, Francis Fraser and Peter Cluness. Front row, from left: Maurice Fraser, Colin Fraser, Tammie Fraser, John Garriock, Mark Anderson and Ivor Moffat.

Photo – Robert Johnson

A memorable day at Lerwick in July 1987 when two new vessels arrive at the same time – the inshore vessel *Diamond* and another *Altaire* for skipper John Peter Duncan and partners.

Photo – Robert Johnson

which had been sold to skipper Winston Watt of Lerwick. His previous vessel, the GRP-hulled *Harvest Gold*, had been sold to a crew in Penzance. John Garriock was in the news again with the third *Sunbeam*, an 87ft long vessel built at Campbeltown at a cost of £1.2 million.

She was the first vessel in Shetland to have her working deck closed entirely with a full length shelter deck. She was the first to have a conveyor system to handle the catch, taking it from the hopper into which the codend had been emptied on the foredeck to sorting and gutting tables, the offal and unwanted species passing out through a chute in the side of the vessel. She was also the first boat in Shetland to have auto-trawl gear. The previous *Sunbeam* was sold to a skipper in Burghead and renamed *Discovery*.

The build up of Shetland's fishing fleet continued in 1987. Another skipper who was climbing up the ladder of progress was Robbie Watt of Lerwick who with his partners acquired the *Andromeda II*, an 87ft long vessel built at St Monans. By this time seine netting was being phased out in the case of larger vessels and the *Andromeda* was equipped solely for trawling. The previous *Andromeda* was sold to a crew from Banff.

The next arrival in Shetland was the islands' first beam trawler, the *Paramount*, formerly the Dutch-owned *Jacob*, bought by skipper Jeemie Anderson and partners. Her stay in Shetland was not a successful one, partly because there was no tradition of this type of fishing in Shetland. More traditional in style was the *Diamond*, a 60ft long seiner/trawler built by Jones of Buckie for skipper Peter Goodlad and his son Angus. She arrived at Lerwick on 8th July, 1987, only a few hours before the arrival of John Peter Duncan's new *Altaire*.

Skipper John David Anderson.

Photo – J. R. Nicolson

During the autumn of 1987 the 53ft *Chelaris* was bought second hand by Ronald Robertson of Yell and towards the end of the year another two Campbeltown 87s were completed for Shetland crews – the *Defiant* (skipper Magnie Stewart) for Whalsay and the *Wave Sheaf* (skipper Tammie Alec Goodlad) for Burra.

Inevitably a number of old vessels left Shetland at this time – the Yell boat *Krisona*; the *Fortuna*, which had been in Whalsay since 1959; and the *Flourish*, owned latterly by Ivor Anderson and partners of Scalloway.

The *Endeavour* fishing west of Shetland.

More vessels arrived in 1988, starting with the *Dee Dawn*, bought second hand by John Umphray and partners of Scalloway. In May the 65ft long *Telstar* was completed by Jones of Buckie for John Scott and partners of Lerwick while in July another Campbeltown 87, the *Alison Kay*, was completed for the John David Anderson and sons of Skerries and the *Endeavour*, yet another Campbeltown 87, arrived for a west side crew headed by Brian Morrison. Another veteran fishing boat, the *Dauntless II*, was sold that year to owners in Buckie and the *Harvest Home* started a new career at Gardenstown.

The catch goes up – and down

As the white fish fleet expanded in the early 1980s there was a sudden rise in the catch of white fish. An example of what the big boats could do with their superior equipment was shown in October 1985 when the *Donvale II* smashed the record for a week's fishing by landing 999½ boxes of fish – mainly haddock and whiting at Scalloway to gross £23,589 for the week. Less than 24 hours later the *Be Ready* took the record with 1084 boxes worth £27,283.

It soon became clear that the bigger catches of this period did not reflect increased stocks of fish but rather the efficiency of their gear and additional horse power. Landings of white fish reached a peak of 18,941 tonnes in 1986 and this was followed by a steady decline in landings, in spite of newer additions to the fleet. Their arrival hastened the end of older vessels with less efficient gear whose catches dropped as the stocks were fished more heavily.

The big boats themselves saw their catches dropping and they solved this problem by developing a new type of trawl, fitted with large rubber discs on the footrope, which enabled them to work on hard bottom for ground fish. The most important species caught with these "rockhoppers" was the monkfish which had previously been thrown back into the sea along with gurnards, "blind hoes" and other trash fish.

There was now a huge demand for monkfish both in the UK and on the Continent. By 1988 landings of monkfish at local markets had reached 1575 tonnes valued at £2.2 million and two years later the catch had reached 2122 tonnes for the year, valued at £3.7 million. There was a huge demand for monks from merchants on the UK mainland and most were shipped out by the P & O ferry to Aberdeen. There is little doubt that without their catches of monks many of the expensive new boats would not have survived.

There were good catches of haddock and whiting in 1986 – 7260 tonnes and 3811 tonnes respectively, but thereafter catches declined until in 1990 the landings of those species at local markets were only 2416 tonnes and 1958 tonnes respectively. Because of the scarcity the average price had risen from £565 per tonne to £1096 per tonne in the case of haddock and from £506 to £752 per tonne in the case of whiting during the same period.

The 1980s had seen the imposition of quotas for each species as the main system of conservation. When the quota for one species was exhausted then that fishery was deemed to have come to an end for that year. The politicians who made that rule seemed to be unaware that fish do not swim in shoals separated according to species, but are a mixture of many species, swimming together, the bigger feeding on the smaller fish at the bottom of the food chain. It was perfectly permissible, when the quota for one species such as haddock was exhausted, to carry on fishing for other species, such as cod and whiting, provided that you dumped all your haddock back into the sea.

There were serious misgivings on the part of Shetland fishermen over the very low allocation of saithe awarded to the Shetland PO, mainly because there had been only a limited market for saithe in Shetland and no incentive to fish directly for this species. Now that Shetland fishermen were anxious to catch saithe because of the scarcity of other species, they were given a very small quota. It was galling for Shetland fishermen to see French trawlers hauling in large saithe while they were having to dump most of their catches.

To dump good fish was against the inborn instinct of fishermen and many of them, throughout the UK, decided to land surplus fish illegally and sell them privately for much less than the market price. This led to the infamous trade in "black" fish, which led to a flood of cheap supplies throughout the country, undermining the price structure at legitimate markets and causing much harm to the industry.

Problems for local processors

White fish processors found it difficult to respond to the changes in the pattern of white fish landings during the 1980s. There was a big rise in catches in 1982 while in January 1983 there was such a scarcity that local firms signed an agreement with British United Trawlers of Grimsby whereby vessels such as the *Ross Tiger* and *Ross Leopard*, which by this time were regarding Shetland as their main fishing ground, would land catches at Scalloway – at least one vessel per week.

In February that year, when the PO was formed, there was a glut of fish and fairly large quantities were being sent to the fish meal factory at Bressay. In March 1983 Young's Shetland Seafoods announced that their plant at Brown's Road, Lerwick was to close with the loss of 25 jobs, although the firm gave an assurance that it would modernise its premises at Holmsgarth. This disappointment was offset by the reopening of the Arlanda factory at Gremista by Shetland Fish Ltd.

The US market, which had declined in importance after 1971 because of adverse exchange rates, staged a recovery in 1982, due to the weakness of the pound and over 1000 tonnes of frozen white fish fillets in laminated blocks were shipped from Scalloway. The recovery continued into 1983 – with help from Shetland Islands Council – leading to renewed optimism throughout the industry.

Council assistance took many forms – loans and equity participation through the agency of the Charitable Trust; lease-back arrangements by means of the council's property company SLAP; a fish processors' fund, originally £50,000 to provide a cushion between the time of shipment and receipt of payment from customers in the USA and Australia, the latter destination having long been an important market for whiting.

In June 1983 the council announced an investment of £1.3 million in L. Williamson (Shetland) Ltd, which by this time had acquired premises in the North of England to add value to its range of products, sold in several parts of the country under the Sheltie trade name.

1984 was another year of change in the white fish processing sector, starting with a change in the system of fish weights when the industry adopted the metric system. The changeover was a simple one without extra expense since the six stone box was now deemed to hold 40kg of fish.

It was a year of considerable progress with the opening of Alting Seafoods' processing plant at Brown's Road, Lerwick, the first new white fish unit to be opened in 12 years. The building was constructed by the SIC's property company SLAP and leased to the processing firm, a partnership of local businessmen with Arthur Nicolson as managing director.

In April the factory at Mid Yell reopened for business under a new company trading as Yell Fisheries. Partners in the venture were Gibby Johnson and four local fishermen. The building was leased from Shetland Islands Council, which had purchased the factory after its closure in 1979.

In 1986 Saga Seafoods, a new company with Willie Henry from Burra as managing director, started work in the old building at Brown's Road, Lerwick, smoking herring and mackerel.

Some significant moves were made in the mid-80s to improve the image of Shetland's seafood industry. In 1985, following visits to Iceland and Norway, sponsored by Shetland Islands Council, the Shetland Seafood Quality Control was set up. Its aim was to improve the quality of Shetland's fish products, starting with the boats themselves – how they handled their catches at sea and on the market – and keeping a careful watch on the product through the processing plants to the ultimate stage of shipment to the customer. Very high standards were required before a fishing boat or processing plant could get the quality mark of the SSQC.

First inspector of the SSQC was an Icelander Leifur Eiriksson, working from an office on the first floor of the Cold Store building at Scalloway. Jim Henry the council's fisheries development officer was secretary of the company and the Shetland PO had a seat on the Board of Directors.

In 1985 the SFA suggested that Shetland should have its own monthly fishing paper. This was launched in November that year as a joint venture with Shetland Fish Processors Association. In the following year the newly formed Shetland Salmon Farmers Association joined the company. The aim of Shetland Fishing News was to provide in-depth coverage of the entire seafood industry in Shetland.

In 1986 local processors set up Shetland Seafare (Marketing) Ltd to co-ordinate the promotion of all the various processors in Shetland. What one firm had done on its own was shown that year by Whalsay Fisheries when it was awarded the Queen's Award for Export Achievement.

None of the moves made at this time to promote the processing industry could conceal the fact that supplies were dwindling at local markets and all firms were working at reduced capacity.

At Scalloway the management of Iceatlantic gave serious consideration to the possibility of extending its herring and mackerel production lines, perhaps processing these species only.

This suggestion was taken up by Shetland Fish Processors Association who realised that if the biggest buyer of white fish was to concentrate solely on herring and mackerel, there would be sufficient supplies of white fish to provide full time working for the others.

The association wrote to Shetland Islands Council, pointing out that in the opinion of its members the processing plant proposed for Lerwick was over ambitious and advising the council to support Iceatlantic in its plans to redevelop the factory at Scalloway.

This suggestion came at an inappropriate time, since the council had set up a pelagic factory action group with representatives of the PO (which had agreed to allocate £500,000 to the project), Lerwick Harbour Trust and the Highlands and Islands Development Board. No one could have foreseen that the end of Iceatlantic was little more than a year away.

As expected the situation with regard to white fish supplies got worse and factories were struggling to survive. During the summer of 1986 Shetland Fish was forced to stop trading, leading to the closure of Arlanda at Lerwick and the factory at Ronas Voe. They did not stay closed for long since they attracted the attention of the Hughes Food Group from Humberside, who acquired the company from the receiver and reopened both plants as Shetland Fish (1986) Ltd.

Few people in Shetland had heard of John Hughes and his company Hughes (Holdings) Ltd. It was known that he was a self-made millionaire who had made a fortune from food processing and dealing in second-hand machinery.

The acquisition of Shetland Fish was just the beginning of Mr Hughes' ambitions in Shetland. He had designs on Iceatlantic, the largest processing plant in Shetland, occupying one of the best possible sites, beside the new harbour at Blacksness.

He approached the main shareholders in the company – the SIC and HIDB – who together owned 70 per cent of the company while the SIC had also purchased the building. When John Hughes approached the main owners he found them eager to sell and so acquired a 90 per cent stake in the company plus a 54 year lease of the factory itself. By this time the HIDB had wound up its fisheries division and a major reorganisation had taken place aimed at making the Board more effective.

At a meeting of the Shetland PO on 18th October, 1986, it was agreed to write to both the council and the HIDB, warning of the danger of having one company in control of 40 per cent of Shetland's white fish processing sector.

The transfer of ownership took place in December 1986 and a few months later the company announced plants to spend £1 million in improving Iceatlantic while doubling its throughput of smoked mackerel and kippered herring to 2500 stones per week.

Only minor improvements were carried out and in a surprise move the firm removed, for sale to a firm in India, the fish meal plant which had been a vital part of the plant's operation since the company started.

The supply of white fish continued to decline and the Hughes Group began to regret its move to Shetland. In June 1987 the Arlanda plant at Lerwick was closed and the employees offered jobs at Iceatlantic, swelling the workforce to 142.

At the end of August that year the company made a serious mistake when it shut down the herring and mackerel smoking operation, claiming that it was "only marginally profitable". The firm continued with its declared intention of building a "super-efficient" white fish operation at Scalloway, which with its satellite at Ronas Voe would be able to handle 3000 boxes of fish each week.

Early in October came the news that the factory at Ronas Voe was to close with the loss of 32 jobs. It did not remain closed for long, its future being secured when the Shetland PO, together with several former employees, successfully negotiated with the Hughes Group to take over the factory. This investment in a white fish processing plant by the Shetland PO complemented the earlier decision to invest in the pelagic factory at Lerwick.

John Goodlad, Chief Executive of the PO had earlier voiced the views of its directors when he said: "The salutary lesson of the closure of Arlanda, Ronas Voe and possibly Iceatlantic is that never again should a non-Shetland company be permitted to acquire such a dominant position in the local fishing industry."

The news that Scalloway had been dreading came in February 1988 when the Hughes Group announced that the factory was to close and that more than 100 workers would be laid off indefinitely. The freezing section remained open to handle offal and sandeels and the company started to process buckies (whelks) for a market in Japan.

In March 1988 it was rumoured that the Hughes Group was considering the possibility of converting the factory to process herring and mackerel on a much larger scale that had been done formerly. It was thought that this plan was connected with the group's spectacular investment in fishing vessels.

As the year advanced it was clear that two firms intended to approach the SIC and HIDB for grants to develop similar processing operations. By this time SPP (Lerwick) Ltd had focused its attention on the former OIL base at Gremista to the north of Lerwick as a suitable site for a modern processing plant.

Both applications were considered by the council's development committee on 30th June, when after a long and often bitter debate it was decided to defer a decision until the next meeting of the committee on 1 August.

That gave the people of Scalloway a chance to get organised, with a Scalloway Development Association and a steering group of 10 members to promote the development of the village, its first aim being to support Iceatlantic in its campaign for a pelagic processing operation.

In this the effort was successful since at the next meeting of the council's development committee it was agreed to offer a grant of £350,000 to Iceatlantic while earmarking a much larger sum – around £2.75 million to SPP.

Both parties then waited for the verdict of the HIDB, which came in a press release on 8th November. It stated that the Board had approved a £242,000 investment package towards the £5 million project at the former OIL base at Lerwick. The Board had earlier emphasised that it would support only one of the two applicants to be "certain of one success rather than two failures".

This left Iceatlantic with the promise of help from the SIC. In spite of this the Hughes Group found it difficult to get backing for its scheme. It seemed at one stage that a joint venture with an Irish company was on the cards but that scheme did not come to fruition and the Hughes Group moved out of Shetland, leaving an empty factory and a cold store which had been allowed to deteriorate through neglect to mark its 2½ years' involvement with Shetland.

The situation was even more desperate for Scalloway since the group retained a 52 year lease on the building. Thanks to the strenuous efforts of Scalloway's councillor Major William A. Anderson, the lease was bought back by the council, thus freeing the site for development some time in the future.

It would be unfair to attach all the blame for this fiasco on the English group. All the processing plants in Shetland were short of fish and by removing the biggest one from the equation the Hughes Group had unwittingly saved some of the others. There was another closure at Scalloway when L. Williamson's plant at Westshore ceased operations, the firm concentrating its activities at Lerwick.

Some firms survived by switching to other species while the rising output of farmed salmon offered alternative opportunities for others.

Salmon farming had started in 1982 and so rapid was the rise in production, by 1987 it had equalled that of white fish with a value of £12 million.

The only conflict with the fishing industry came when a salmon farm threatened inshore fishing grounds. In 1985 the SFA appealed against a decision by the Shetland Islands Council to grant permission to farm salmon in Busta Voe on valuable queen scallop grounds. Although the association lost the appeal to the Secretary of State a victory was gained insofar as the Secretary of State recommended that the council should in future consult fully with the association with regard to the siting of salmon farms.

In 1987 Alting Seafoods switched to processing salmon and Saga Seafoods did likewise. The Arlanda factory was reopened in 1988 by Will Wyllie and John Wood to fillet monkfish, skate and flatfish for a fresh fish market in the UK. The fresh fish market also gave a brief respite to Williamsons' plant at Scalloway when operated by Pioneer Seafoods. Cash flow problems and bad debts on the continent eventually brought this activity to an end.

Haddock and whiting were not the only species to cause concern in the 1980s – the catch of sandeels also dropped alarmingly. When this fishery was blamed for the breeding failures of seabirds, environmental groups called for an investigation. It was clear that plunge-feeding birds such as kittiwakes and arctic terns had failed to raise their young because their main food, the sandeels, had been depleted.

A seminar held in the Shetland Hotel on 15th and 16th October, 1988, confirmed that the main reason for the seabird breeding failures was the scarcity of sandeels, but it failed to prove that the fishery had caused this crisis. Nevertheless it recorded the steady rise of this fishery from its start in 1974, after which the catch rose to a peak of 52,000 tonnes in 1982, and its collapse to a low point of 4800 tonnes in 1988.

As a result of the seminar it was agreed to carry out detailed research into the biology of the sandeel, its distribution around Shetland and the various factors which could have contributed to its decline.

While the annual dinner dance was always a special occasion for the SFA, that of 7th November, 1987, was of unusual importance since it marked its 40th anniversary.

In his speech after the meal its secretary John Goodlad traced the origins of the association from its beginnings in the early part of the century to the start of a formal organisation in 1947 and the success achieved since then.

In spite of all the ups and downs the association was in a strong position with a total of 98 vessels in membership – nine pelagic vessels, 34 shellfish boats and a large fleet of 46 white fish vessels, some of them the most modern in the UK.

Training Shetland's fishermen

Navigation and seamanship had been taught in some Shetland schools for generations, as the first step for young men to obtain mates' and masters' tickets for the Merchant Navy and helping young men to obtain the qualifications required to serve as skipper on the bigger fishing boats (including steam drifters) in the local fleet.

Since the second world war greater importance has been attached to training within the fishing industry and much of the credit for the very high standard achieved locally in the 1960s and 1970s must go to the late Janette

Williamson, a teacher at Symbister House Secondary School in Whalsay, who obtained her yacht master's certificate (foreign going) to enable her to teach navigation.

Around 80 fishermen attended her classes over the years and all of them gained certificates of competency, which played a great part in the development of Shetland's fishing industry at that time. Her achievements were recognised with the award of the MBE in 1972.

Another teacher who played a part in this sector of education was Tom Moncrieff of Lerwick, who taught navigation at Lerwick Central School in the 1970s with special classes for fishermen.

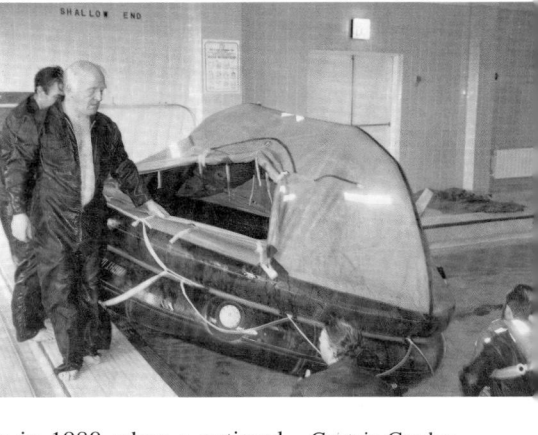

Captain Gordon Walterson supervising a life saving course in the old Lerwick swimming pool.

Photo – J. R. Nicolson

An important step in training nationally came in 1980 when a national Fisheries Training Council was set up under Ken Waind, later taken over by the Sea Fish Industry Authority and the forerunner in the industry of the YTS and YT schemes which came later.

Mr Waind met representatives of the association to encourage improved training provision for Shetland fishermen. As a result of those meetings the association established the Shetland Fishermen's Training Association in 1981. Captain Gordon Walterson from Sandness was appointed training co-ordinator. A room for training was provided at the Anderson High School; but soon afterwards the association was informed that it would have to find other premises since that room was required for oboe lessons.

The fact that Shetland's principal educational establishment appeared to give music lessons a much greater priority than the training of the next generation of fishermen galvanised the local industry into a campaign to ensure that much better provision was made for the training of Shetland's fishermen. As a first step classes moved from the Anderson High School to the former canteen at the "old" Lerwick Central School and from there to wartime huts at Brown's Road. Although barely adequate these were to serve for several years.

An engineering class at Brown's Road, Lerwick. From left: Stuart Anderson, Harry Sandison, Mark Davies, Martin Hay, Christopher Duncan, John Montgomery and instructor Cecil Duncan.

Photo – J. R. Nicolson

Captain Walterson was assisted by a number of dedicated men who provided tuition in their respective skills – like Jeemie Smith of H. Williamson & Sons in electronics, Charlie Hunter and Jeemsie Ward in net mending and John Pottinger, Cecil Duncan and Tammie W. Laurenson in engineering.

Those taking their tickets had to attend colleges on the mainland, while in 1979 the practice began of attending the sea school at Stromness in Orkney under Captain Robbie Sutherland.

Captain Walterson retired in 1991 and the remit of training co-ordinator was widened to include coverage of fish processing and fish farming with Jim Tait and George Hunter holding the post jointly, while the organisation was renamed Shetland Fisheries Training Association.

The first official recognition of the need for a fisheries training college in Shetland came in 1979 when John Goodlad published his Shetland Fishing Plan. The suggestion was taken up by Dr Alistair Goodlad in 1984 in his report on the future of the fishing industry in Shetland and soon afterwards a steering group was formed to consider the proposal.

The Shetland Islands Council played an important role in the discussions and sponsored visits to training establishments in Iceland, Faroe, Norway and the Scottish mainland. On a visit to Banff and Buchan College of Further Education, Captain Forbes Watt, Head of the Nautical Department, gave invaluable advice on the planning and construction of a fisheries college with involvement by both industry and local government. His prediction that the programme would take ten years was greeted with scepticism but he was proved right.

The steering group identified three sites which might be suitable for this development – at Symbister House Secondary School in Whalsay, near the coastguard station at Lerwick and at Port Arthur, Scalloway, on the site of a former herring curing station.

While each site had its merits and its supporters, councillor William A. Anderson pointed out that the Scalloway site had an added advantage in that the council was already the owner of the land. He was successful in persuading his fellow councillors that for this and other reasons Scalloway was the preferred location.

Another steering group was formed, consisting of representatives of Shetland Islands Council, Shetland Fishermen's Association, Shetland Fish Processors' Association and the Shetland Salmon Farmers' Association, with councillor Willie Cumming as chairman. By this time it had been agreed that the project should be co-ordinated by the council's Department of Research and Development and that the Department of Design and Technical Services should begin work on outline plans for a building which was expected to cost £1.5 million.

In December 1988 a trust was formed to administer the proposed training college, with council convener Edward Thomason as chairman. A Board of Management was also set up with councillor William A. Anderson as chairman.

The next major step came in October 1989 when Dr Jessie Watt was appointed co-ordinator of the project, her remit being to liaise with all the various groups involved, including the architects, and to investigate all possible sources of funding.

Site preparations by the council's construction department started in the summer of 1990 with the demolition of an old building used originally as a kippering kiln. At the same time thousands of tonnes of rock were being transported from the Scord Quarry as infill to extend the site seawards. It was not until 28th November, 1990, that the council finally gave the go-ahead for this project which was now expected to cost £5.9 million. Construction work

started in December 1990, the contract having been awarded to local firm DITT Construction.

The North Atlantic Fisheries College officially opened in 1994.

Preparations for the college led to a new use for the suite of offices in the redundant Iceatlantic building, as Dr Watt took over one of the offices in November 1990. Within a few weeks she was joined by Martin Holmes as he prepared modular courses in aquaculture, and Captain Stuart Yeamans, who was appointed head of nautical studies.

Courses in aquaculture started in the summer of 1991 in a room in Scalloway Public Hall, while laboratory work was carried out in Scalloway school. Classes for fishermen started in the Iceatlantic offices, the first three students being Michael Watt and Alex Simpson of Lerwick and Kevin Ritch of Yell, as they studied for Class Two certificates of competency. All of them passed their exams, getting the fledgling college off to a good start.

The next appointment came in August 1991 when Mark Jeffrey was appointed lecturer in engineering. He was followed by Gordon Johnson, an assistant in the department of nautical studies and in February 1992 Captain Robert Sinclair was appointed principal of the college.

While the college was getting under way more valuable advice and assistance came from Captain Forbes Watt after he retired from his post as head of the nautical department at the Banff and Buchan College of Further Education.

The number of students rose steadily over the next few years and before long the college was attracting students from several parts of the world, as its reputation grew, confirming the predictions of those who had worked so hard to make it a success.

The North Atlantic Fisheries College was opened officially on Monday 25th April, 1994, by Jack Burgess, who as head of the council's Department of Research and Development had done so much hard work in bringing this project to a successful completion.

CHAPTER EIGHT

The success of Shetland Catch

After many months of discussion, SPP (Lerwick) Ltd agreed to proceed with its plans for a modern pelagic processing plant at Lerwick. In September 1988 the project was entrusted to the care of civil engineers Arch Henderson & Partners, who had done an enormous amount of work in Shetland over the years. The firm's remit was to provide a modern high production fish processing plant, built to the highest standard of hygiene and conforming to the latest EEC rules.

It was stipulated in the contract that the plant should be completed and commissioned by July 1989, in time for that summer's herring fishery.

The contract to convert the existing warehouse into the factory's production hall and chill and to upgrade the existing office block went to local firm DITT. Equipment for the 3000 tonne cold store, the chilled area, the blast freezers and vertical plate freezers was supplied by Refrigeration (Aberdeen) Ltd.

A major contract, worth over £600,000 went to the Icelandic group Icecon, to supply conveyor systems and grading and processing lines from Meka and weighing systems from Marel, while German firm Baader supplied filleting and skinning machines.

The factory, thereafter known as Shetland Catch, was designed to produce herring flaps, fillets and skinless fillets as well as whole fish, frozen for further processing by customers in various parts of the world.

The only part of the operation which was not fully automated was the system for transporting fish from the quay to the chilled reception area. Here the company was to rely for several years on plastic bins moved by forklifts and trucks.

The first full time employee was David Fullerton, a partner in JFM (Electrical and Refrigeration) who became responsible for the maintenance of all the electrical and refrigeration equipment in the factory. The factory was ready for a test run on 2nd July, 1989, when it purchased two tonnes of herring from the Swedish purse seiner *Astrid*. This allowed final adjustments to be made. A few days later Shetland Catch had its first commercial landing of 12 tonnes of herring from the local purse seiner *Azalea*.

Shetland Catch was fortunate in building up an excellent workforce under its manager Dick Wailes, many of the employees, including assistant manager Jim Ridland, having had years of experience at Iceatlantic. During the early years of Shetland Catch management was provided under contract by Whalsay Fisheries with Bobby McLeod playing a key role along with Mr Wailes.

While Shetland Catch made a big contribution to the success of that summer's fishery at Lerwick, the main outlet was still the Eastern Bloc klondykers which reached a peak of 40 vessels and purchased 43,860 tonnes. Shetland Catch handled 1933 tonnes and 2395 tonnes went for fish meal.

The only disappointment that year was the collapse of the market for herring roe, the factory having been prepared to pay £160 per tonne for full herring. Japan had gone into mourning after the death of Emperor Hirohito and luxuries like herring roe were off the menu for the time being.

The official opening of Shetland Catch was performed on Saturday 9th September, 1989, by council vice-convener Willie Tait, deputising for convener Edward Thomason who was unwell. Adding a touch of glamour to the occasion was Miss World, Linda Petursdottir from Iceland, who unveiled a plaque to mark the occasion.

There was good news from John Goodlad who announced that the Scottish Office had agreed to Lerwick's request to become recognised as a transhipping port for mackerel for the first time. The EEC had conceded that the western mackerel stock was staying longer in the sea area west of 4 degrees west.

The UK quota for the coming season had been set at 190,500 tonnes of which 35,790 tonnes could be caught east of the 4 degree line and of this 30,000 tonnes could be discharged at Lerwick between 1st October and 31st December.

The harbour authority at Peterhead was bitterly disappointed that its application for a share of the catch had been refused and there was disappointment too at Ullapool that the winter klondyking operation which had brought such prosperity to the town, at an otherwise quiet time of year, was to be shared with another port.

As the herring season merged into the mackerel season Shetland Catch remained busy right through the autumn. By the end of October it became clear that the 30,000 tonnes allocated to Lerwick would soon be exhausted and the Government issued a notice ordering that the fishery should close on Saturday 4th November.

John Peter Duncan, skipper of the *Altaire*, meets Miss World, Linda Petursdottir, at the opening of Shetland Catch.

As if in defiance of the Government, the fleet encountered dense shoals of mackerel on the night of 3rd November and every vessel arrived in port with a large catch, which boosted Lerwick's total to 40,000 tonnes and set the seal on an excellent year for the port.

For Shetland's fishing industry as a whole it was a record year with fish landings valued at £23.08 million compared with £16.33 million the previous year. The rise was due solely to an increase in the quantity of mackerel landed or transhipped at Lerwick – up from 1065 tonnes worth £74,872 in 1988 to 47,778 tonnes valued at £5.45 million in 1989. There was a drop in the catch of white fish from 14,230 tonnes to 12,399 tonnes while the value remained roughly the same at around £10.8 million.

There was a slow start to the herring season of 1990 because the Eastern Bloc klondykers refused to pay the EEC minimum price fixed for July. They waited until August when the price dropped to £112.42 per tonne and then the fishery got under way.

Thereafter the build-up was rapid, reaching a peak of 44 klondykers – 23 from Russia and the Baltic states, six Polish, five Romanian, five Bulgarian, four Dutch and a single East German.

Towards the end of August, as the herring filled prior to spawning, a fair proportion of the catch was bought by Japanese firms for the traditional roe market, freezing being carried out on the klondykers.

The klondykers
from the Eastern
Bloc.

Photo – Kieran
Murray

The klondykers
from the Eastern
Bloc.

Photo – Kieran
Murray

Once again the factory ships took most of the catch – a total of 38,000 tonnes – while 4400 tonnes went for fish meal. Shetland Catch processed 3500 tonnes from UK vessels and around 1000 tonnes from Faroese vessels, which enabled the factory to operate during July. Shetland Catch had a second production line that year, having leased part of the Iceatlantic plant at Scalloway to produce spiced and vinegar-cured herring. Around 2700 barrels of the former and 900 barrels of the latter were filled for markets in Sweden

A major cause for concern that summer was the threat hanging over the fish meal plant at Bressay, still owned and operated by the Norwegian firm Herring By-Products. It was a vital part of the herring trade at Lerwick, being able to absorb the fish which other outlets could not handle. It had suffered a severe decline in landings of Norway pout, while landings of sand-eels were now limited to those coming from outwith the Shetland area.

Loading up the large
bin from the hopper.

Photo – J. R.
Nicolson

Fortunately a local consortium, Shetland Fish Products Ltd, was formed to acquire the plant. Half the shares were held by United Fish Products of Aberdeen, the other partners being Shetland Fish Processors Association (15 per cent), Shetland Catch, the Shetland Fish Producers Organisation (10 per cent) and Lerwick Harbour Trust (10 per cent) and the Shetland Norse Fish Farm (5 per cent). As part of the deal Lerwick Harbour Trust acquired the quays and quayside equipment. Yet again the fishermen of Shetland had become involved in another fish processing venture of vital importance to their primary activity.

After improvements to the plant Shetland Fish Products Ltd started working in March 1991, handling catches of blue whiting from British and Scandinavian vessels and sandeels from vessels working on west coast grounds.

By this time it had become clear that the mackerel fishery was of greater importance to Shetland than the herring fishery. While the demand for herring had weakened there was still a keen demand for mackerel, especially in the Soviet Union.

The mackerel fishery continued to present problems for those administering it, because of a continuing change in the

Transferring the catch to the klondyker.

Photo – J. R. Nicolson

movement of the shoals. From 1990 onwards they were staying longer within the Norwegian sector of the North Sea, before starting the migration to spawning grounds west of Ireland. This created a headache for those whose job it was to calculate how much could be caught within each sector within a specified time. Part of the problem centred on the longitudinal line of 4 degrees west, the bureaucratic division between the two areas, each with a different quota.

In 1990 Lerwick was allocated a total of 18,000 tonnes for klondyking, compared with 30,000 tonnes the previous year. The reduction was necessary since the harbour authorities at Aberdeen, Peterhead and Fraserburgh all

The huge size of the klondykers can be guaged from the size of the fishing vessels alongside.

Photo – J. Coutts

wanted a share of the klondyking activity. In a letter to the fisheries department John Goodlad pointed out that while Lerwick had been playing host to the entire klondyking fleet for a month, not a single klondyker had appeared at any of the Scottish ports. The department accepted this argument and Lerwick was awarded a further 10,000 tonnes.

A new trophy marking the achievements of the late Henry Stewart, councillor for Whalsay and Skerries, was awarded for the first time in 1990 to the purse seiner landing the best quality herring and mackerel as seen in the average price. First winner was the *Serene* (skipper Bobby Polson) with an average of £133.13 per tonne.

That was the year when the directors of Shetland Catch realised that their plant was only one of a number of such factories around the rim of the North Sea, all competing for supplies, as Shetland vessels were attracted to outlets in Norway and Denmark where the price for mackerel was as high as £300 per tonne.

In November 1990 the Scottish Office called a halt to klondyking at Lerwick and directed the vessels to Ullapool, even though the mackerel were still in the Shetland area, involving long and sometimes dangerous journeys to the west coast port by vessels deeply loaded and in heavy seas.

The politicians were beginning to accept that the mackerel had indeed altered their migratory pattern and agreed that a greater share of the catch

An impressive sight – the Shetland Catch factory with some of the Shetland pelagic fleet berthed at the pier.

could be taken in the North Sea. In 1971 Lerwick's share was increased to 45,000 tonnes to be landed between 1st October and 31st December, or until the quota was taken.

In 1992 mackerel overtook herring as the species with the biggest tonnage landed at Lerwick – 59,274 tonnes worth £7.3 million, compared with 37,396 tonnes of herring valued at £4.8 million. White fish was still the most valuable sector with 10,505 tonnes worth £10.86 million.

The end of December still marked the klondyking transition from Lerwick to Ullapool, which led to severe problems for fishermen during winter storms. Some had to cut short their voyage to Ullapool and head for Lerwick, when the catch had deteriorated so much that it was suitable only for fish meal. The Department was forced to recognise the reality of the situation and granted a further extension of the season at Lerwick.

The mackerel shoals appeared later every year. In the autumn of 1993 Shetland Catch and the klondykers were idle for long periods or at best underutilised. Then in January 1994 the fleet brought in 40,000 tonnes, almost equal to the catch of the pervious three months. The Department closed the port for transhipment at midnight on Wednesday 2nd February.

The most important event that year was the arrival of the new *Altaire*. She was 243 feet long with a 6000hp engine and she was equipped solely for trawling. Like her predecessors she had been built in Norway.

In 1994 the autumn fishery got of to a dismal start as fishermen spent most of November tied up in port rather than spending long periods at sea searching for the shoals, burning fuel and finding nothing. While Shetland Catch managed to maintain full production, the klondykers were idle and some moved elsewhere to find work. By the end of the month their numbers had dropped from 90 to 50.

In the first week of January 1995 25 arrivals brought in 5480 tonnes. The next few days could have provided bumper catches as dense shoals were found to the west of Shetland; but bad weather intervened and when conditions improved the mackerel were nearer Ullapool. While the smaller Shetland boats landed their catches there the bigger boats headed for Norway or Denmark, being paid as much as £320 per tonne.

Lerwick was exceptionally busy in the early 1990s thanks to the extended activity of the herring and mackerel fisheries. In 1989 Shetland became the top fishery district in the UK with 123,000 tonnes of fish landed or transhipped. Peterhead came next with 101,000 tonnes and Ullapool, which had been the top port for several years, was third with 97,000 tonnes. Because of the higher prices paid for white fish Peterhead was top as regards value with landings worth £68 million; Aberdeen was second with £27 million and Shetland was third with £23 million according to the Sea Fisheries statistics for that year.

The klondykers were an important part of the local economy. Their clumsy looking lifeboats called daily to load supplies, crowding into the berths reserved for them at the north-west corner of Victoria Pier, and off-duty crewmen and women came ashore for shopping.

The Russians were relatively well paid, unlike the Poles and Bulgarians who had to trade at the lower end of the market. Nothing was wasted in Lerwick in those days, as electrical goods due for the scrapyard were

The Russian lifeboats loading up with supplies.

Photo – J. R. Nicolson

Continual development – the new discharge facility at Shetland Catch.

taken home to be repaired and little of any value was left in the rubbish skips at the town's rubbish dumps.

Viking Sea Taxis had the old MFV type vessel *Zenobia* maintaining a shuttle service between Lerwick and the klondykers. Because of the numbers involved very few of these vessels were allocated spaces within Lerwick Harbour. Most klondykers had to anchor north of Bressay or near the south entrance of the harbour. Inevitably when gales were forecast most of these had to head for the open sea and dodge out of the storm.

There were several emergencies during those years which tested to the full the ability of the local rescue services. The most dramatic incidents involved the Latvian vessel *Lunokhod I*, wrecked near the Bressay lighthouse on 9th November, 1993, and the Russian ship *Borodinskoye Polye*, wrecked on the Unicorn a week later.

In the case of the Latvian vessel the Shetland Coastguard rescue helicopter based at Sumburgh winched 56 of the crew to safety, ferrying them in two trips to Lerwick, where they were taken into the care of the local Fishermen's Mission. In the other incident Lerwick lifeboat, under coxswain Hewitt Clark, rescued 37 crewmen, running in 35 times to pick up one or two people from the foot of a rope ladder. The remaining 36 were taken off by the helicopter.

In spite of so many people from different parts of Europe gathering at Lerwick for the herring and mackerel seasons during those years, there was very little trouble. They were a credit to their ships and to the countries from which they came. There is little doubt that the friendship shown to them while in Shetland played a significant part in the improvement in relations between those countries and the UK in subsequent years.

CHAPTER NINE

White fish stocks in trouble

After a long period of expansion Shetland's white fish catch showed a severe drop in the late 1980s – from 17,000 tonnes worth £12.66 million in 1987 to 14,230 tonnes worth £10.84 million the following year.

The gravity of the situation became clear when scientists recommended a reduction in the annual catch of haddock from EU waters to 50,000 tonnes and in the cod catch to 113,000 tonnes. Fisheries Commissioner Sr Manuel Marin reacted by stating that these figures should be cut still further to 31,000 tonnes and 35,000 tonnes respectively. Association secretary John Goodlad pointed out that this would amount to only eight boxes of haddock and 10 boxes of cod per boat each week.

As an alternative to quotas the association had produced its own recommendations for conserving fish stocks. These included an increase in the minimum mesh size in trawls and seine nets; an increase in the minimum landing sizes of haddock and whiting; and a ban on attachments to nets which effectively made the meshes smaller.

The SFA had long maintained that the surest way to conserve stocks was to reduce fishing effort by a decommissioning scheme, with grants being made available to those who wanted to leave the industry and scrap their boats.

It had been calculated that the total cost of decommissioning all white fish vessels over 25 years old in the UK fleet would be £64 million, of which half would be met by the EEU.

In March 1990 the UK Government announced its own measures for conserving fish stocks. It divided the fleet into two categories. In category A were those which had caught less than 40 tonnes of haddock in 1989 and those for whom haddock accounted for less than 10 per cent of their catch of all species. These vessels would be allowed to fish for as many days as they wished, provided that they did not catch more than two thirds of the weight of haddock taken the previous year.

In category B were the remaining vessels (except those under 10m long, all of which were outwith the licensing scheme). Vessels in category B could fish unrestricted if they used a net with a mesh size of 110m, otherwise they would be restricted to 92 days for the remainder of the year.

At the same time the Government introduced changes in the licensing system. The new regulations allowed fishermen to transfer licences from more than one vessel to a new larger one, provided that the capacity of the new vessel must not amount to more than 90 per cent of the total capacity of the vessels it replaced, as calculated by a formula which took into account both vessel size and horse power. Prior to those regulations there were no restrictions on the size of vessel joining the UK fleet. The new licensing system introduced a small degree of restriction whereas previously there had been none.

In spite of the restrictions imposed 1990 was a record year for Shetland, when landings by UK vessels reached a total value of £24.79 million. The white fish sector was again the most valuable with a catch of 11,386 tonnes worth £12.8 million compared with 12,399 tonnes valued at £10.79 million the previous year.

The Government tried a different approach the following year with a tie-up of eight consecutive days each month from February 1991, affecting those vessels over 10m long, when catches from 1st January, 1989, to 30th June, 1990, contained more than 40 per cent of cod and haddock from the North Sea and west of Scotland grounds. Boats that had caught less than 100 tonnes from those areas were excluded and all boats would be exempt from these regulations if they were prepared to use 110mm nets and the added conservation measure of square mesh panels. Twenty-six local boats were affected by the regulations and 17 were exempt because of their low catches of cod and haddock.

These proposals were discussed by the association on 21st December, 1990, and rejected as unjust and unworkable. It was pointed out that fishermen would be forced to go to sea during bad weather to make up for time lost during the tie-up. The association reiterated its view on the matter, adding to the original proposals a ban on the landing of ungutted fish and an increase in the minimum landing sizes. During the previous year the islands council had chartered the white fish trawler *Sunbeam* to carry out a series of experiments, using different combinations of 90mm nets fitted with 80mm square mesh panels. These proved conclusively that such panels allowed a high proportion of immature fish to escape.

The Government noted the effectiveness of experiments such as these and in March 1991 it announced that most white fish vessels would have to fit 90mm square mesh panels in their nets from 1st July. Exceptions were made for boats fishing with diamond meshes over 100mm and those with engines under 400hp.

Unfortunately square mesh panels were never introduced because the vast majority of vessels continued to use diamond meshes over 100mm incorporating double twine. In reality the double twine 100mm diamond mesh was less selective than the 90mm square mesh panel. Since then the association has continued to argue for the mandatory introduction of a 90mm square mesh panel for vessels over 500hp and 80mm square mesh panel for vessels with engines under 500hp.

In October 1991, during the ten year review of the Common Fisheries Policy, the SFA opened an office in Brussels so that its secretary John Goodlad could be on hand when major issues such as effort limitation, mesh size increases, decommissioning, western mackerel flexibility, TACs and quotas were being discussed. Its principal aim, however was still to promote the Shetland Box licensing scheme.

The opening of its own office in Brussels was a major landmark for the association. It demonstrated how political the fishing industry had become and also indicated how professional the association had become in that, by itself, it could establish, fund and staff an office in Brussels. The office remained open until February 1992.

The success of this venture became clear when, following the 10 year review of the CFP, the Shetland Box became firmly established as a permanent feature of European fishing policy. An added bonus was that Shetland was included as part of the Objective One preferential grant scheme, in so far as fisheries projects were concerned. The days at sea regulations were tightened still further in 1992, when boats subject to those constraints would have to stay in port for 135 days in the 12 months from 1st February, under a new EU conservation package.

At the same time the Government issued a consultation paper seeking comments on a number of possible measures designed to aid conservation. These included a ban on the landing of ungutted fish, the continued compulsory use of square mesh panels and a ban on ropes and other attachments to nets.

The SFA Executive Committee 1991 – back row, left to right: John Scott, John Anderson, John David Henry, Francis Hawkins, David Anderson and Alistair Thomason. Middle row: Brian Morrison, Peter Jamieson, Arthur Polson, Brian Isbister, Leslie Tait and Johnnie Sales. Front row: John Goodlad, Mackie Polson, Dr Jessie Watt, Henry Stewart, John Garriock and John Arthur Simpson.

Photo – John Coutts

At its meeting on 8th February, 1992, the SFA welcomed these proposals, especially the one calling for a ban on the landing of ungutted fish – something that the association had been advocating for years.

Unfortunately the Government did not introduce a ban on the landing of ungutted fish. It was prevented from doing so by the widespread opposition from certain sectors of the British fishing industry.

However the Government accepted the validity of another measure long advocated by the association when it introduced a decommissioning scheme worth £25 million, to be spread over two years.

It also proposed changes in the licensing system so that when a licence was transferred a further reduction in the capacity of the vessel would be achieved. This was part of a wider scheme to reduce the size of the fleet as demanded by the EU under its Multi-Annual Guidance Programme (MAGP).

The Government also introduced a rule which allowed POs to buy and sell quotas and to buy out any of their members who wanted to leave the industry. The Shetland PO was the first in Britain to take advantage of this rule and since 1993 it has purchased almost 4000 tonnes of white fish quota. As well as providing generous quotas for Shetland vessels, this pool of quota has also been used to encourage new entrants into the fishing industry.

A tough new set of rules came into operation on 1st June, 1992, whereby the standard mesh size of trawls and seine nets was raised from 90mm to 100mm with exceptions for boats fishing for whiting. A new net rule was introduced to stop fishermen using a 70mm net to catch white fish on the pretext of using it for prawns.

The prospects for 1993 were bleak as the EU threatened to introduce a tie-up of 190 days on the basis of ten consecutive day periods, in addition to the UK Government's tie-up scheme. There was therefore great relief when the end-of-year Fisheries Council at Brussels voted against the proposed tie-up scheme.

Moreover virtually all the white fish and pelagic quotas of interest to the Shetland fleet were increased, the most dramatic increase being in the case of haddock, while the increase in the mackerel TAC would give the Shetland PO a quota of more than 50,000 tonnes for the first time.

Commenting on the end of year negotiations SFA secretary John Goodlad remarked: "I feel we have turned the corner."

The effect on the fishing fleet

These problems in the white fish sector resulted in greater pressure on the shellfish stocks. With poor returns from trawling and seine netting some of the bigger boats, like the *Radiant Star* and *Unison*, switched to scallop fishing. Jeemie Robb of Scalloway acted in much the same way when early in 1989 he sold his white fish vessel *Trident* and replaced her with the smaller shellfish boat *Capella*. Some fishermen still had faith in the future of the white fish sector – like the crew from Yell who brought the 77ft long *Discovery* back to Shetland. She had been built in 1980 as the *Sunbeam*.

Another shellfish boat which arrived at this time was the *Renown*, a Cygnus boat with a GRP hull, bought by John William Anderson of Skerries, while the steel-hulled *Sondra* was built at the Malakoff yard for Colin and John Eunson of Whalsay at a cost of £200,000. Another addition to the Yell fleet was the steel-hulled *Kiaull Marrey*, bought by brothers Leslie and Michael Gray.

1990 was a year which showed again the dangers inherent in fishing. Early in January a young fisherman, Ewan Sutherland from Gulberwick, a crewman on the *Alison Kay*, was drowned in Lerwick harbour. In May David Gear, originally from Foula, was drowned when the *Betula* sank after its scallop dredges had come fast. In September Roderick MacIntyre died while diving for scallops from the fishing boat *Integrity* off Kirk Holm, south of Sand. Another tragedy marred the final weeks of the year when the Inverness registered *Premier* capsized in a storm and sank with her six crewmen only 30 miles east of Lerwick.

There were more changes in the local fleet. Early in 1990 the Skerries boat *Comet* was sold to a crew from Ireland. She had arrived in 1971 for skipper Jackie Hughson and partners. In June 1990 the 9.99m long *Brilliant* (LK 1) – the second of this name – arrived for Michael Watt and Thomas Herridge. She was the first boat in Shetland to have a seawater tank incorporated in her hull for keeping shellfish alive. Another addition to the shellfish fleet that year was the steel-hulled *Shahdaroba* for Philip Johnson of Burra and David Sutherland of Dunrossness.

Brothers Leslie and Michael Gray had an alarming experience when the *Kiaull Marrey* sank off Burravoe on 26th March. They were rescued by the Whalsay boat *Sondra* and their vessel was replaced by the smaller vessel *Sincere V*.

More additions were made to the fleet in 1991. In June the 39ft long shellfish boat *Harvester* was bought by Bruce Anderson and his brother Robert John, both of Whalsay, while in July another shellfish boat, the *Kestrel II* was bought by Bruce Watt of Trondra.

The event which caused the greatest amount of excitement that year was the return of the old Fifie *Swan*, after being bought by the Swan Trust for restoration, being restored over the next few years to her original design as a smack-rigged vessel. Shetland Fishermen's Association was one of a large number of local organisations which made a financial contribution towards the cost of restoration.

It was another year of dramatic incidents, starting with the loss of the Inverness registered *Valkyrie* which ran aground and sank off Bressay,

Considered a big boat in her day, the restored sailing Fifie *Swan* noses past the deep water trawler *Andromeda III*.

Photo – J. R. Nicolson

fortunately without loss of life. Brothers Stanley and Stephen Gray had a narrow escape when the *Argonaut* sank on 28th April north-east of Papa Stour. After several hours in their life-raft they were rescued by the Aith lifeboat *Snolda*. In June the Whalsay boat *Lizanne* snagged her gear on a seabed obstruction and sank, her crew being rescued by the *Renown*.

In October there was talk of a "Fetlar triangle" when two boats went down near the island. On the 16th of the month the *Freedom* caught fire and sank, her crewmen Russell Smith and Stanley Gray being picked up by a fast rescue craft from the oilfield standby vessel *Far Sky*.

A week later the shellfish boat *Chelaris* began to fill with water and sank. Brothers John and Victor Robertson were picked up by the coastguard rescue helicopter.

The *Freedom* was replaced by a bigger boat, the Montrose registered *Whispering Hope* which had once been based at Scalloway as the *Planet*.

The search for new species

As familiar stocks of white fish became scarce there was renewed interest in locating and marketing species which in general had been ignored by local fishermen. In April 1990 the purse seiner *Altaire* went after blue whiting and arrived at Lerwick, low in the water, with 1500 tonnes on board. Two weeks later she broke her own record when she landed 2246 tonnes of blue whiting at a fish meal plant in Faroe.

She then went in search of argentines, a species which, it was hoped, might provide opportunities for local processing firms. The experiment was a failure, the *Altaire* catching only two tonnes in two trips.

In May 1990 the stern trawler *Vega* was chartered by Shetland Islands Council to carry out an experiment in deep water west of the UK to investigate the potential of deep water species which French fishermen had been catching – and marketing – for several years. Her two landings at Scalloway attracted a great deal of attention, as strange fish with unfamiliar names like rat tails, red directors, grenadiers, darkie charlies and red scabbard were offered for sale.

Unfortunately the merchants were not impressed and most of the fish went for fish meal, apart from samples bought by Shetland Catch for further appraisal. The Lerwick factory also purchased 60 tonnes of blue whiting on one occasion.

The Lerwick fish marketing company Framgord saw an opportunity for local firms in southern blue whiting, caught by trawlers off New Zealand and frozen at sea. A consignment of 64 tonnes was loaded at Christchurch, brought in refrigerated containers to Tilbury, thence by road to Aberdeen and finally by P & O to Lerwick. The consignment was given to L. Williamson and Ronas Fisheries to be processed to Framgord's own specifications.

Framgord had had a phenomenal rise to become a major force in Shetland's fisheries. The firm was started in June 1986 by Frank Johnson and Frank Odie to market fish in the USA on behalf of processing firms in Shetland, Orkney, Scotland and Scandinavia. Its principal activity was marketing salmon and its rise was so rapid that within two years its turnover was half a million pounds a week.

The monkfish was still the most valuable species for local white fish trawlers but becoming scarcer as the fishery intensified, in spite of the steady procession by local vessels into deeper water.

Scarcest of all was the halibut, once common around Shetland. In September 1988 the two-man crew of the Scalloway boat *Pilot Us*, which used to get good catches with its longlines, spent two weeks setting lines in all the favoured places without catching a single halibut.

Whenever a halibut was caught by a trawler there was a keen demand for it. In October 1990 the *Sunbeam* set up a record for Shetland with a 16 stone halibut which was sold to Pioneer Seafoods for £453.

With the shortage of haddock and whiting Ronas Fisheries found an outlet for salted ling, a species which was once the mainstay of the fishing industry in Northmavine, during the period of the open boat haaf fishing in the 18th and 19th centuries.

In 1990 Pioneer Seafoods, whose main activity was processing scallops and queen scallops, began processing monks and other high value species for fresh fish markets in the UK and on the continent. Processors of shellfish found a competitor in 1990 when the Spanish firm Airmar had a truck with vivier tanks travelling once a week from Shetland to La Caruna in Spain.

Some of the most successful ventures of this period involved types of gear which had proved their efficiency elsewhere. In May 1991 automatic jigging machines made by DNG in Iceland were tried by skipper Jeemie Robb of Scalloway in the *White Heather* (ex-*Capella*) and by Jim Smith of Yell in the *Aquarius*. While the *White Heather* with two machines was operating independently, the *Aquarius* with six machines was sponsored by Shetland Islands Council. This proved to be the most successful of all council sponsored experiments, moving to the commercial stage very quickly. In a three day period at the end of May the *Aquarius* caught 60 boxes of cod which sold for over £3000.

Jim Smith of Burravoe, a pioneer in jigging for cod.

Photo – Jim Henry

Another two boats, the *Winsome* (Konrad Flaws) and the *Freedom* (Russell Smith) confirmed suspicions that there could be a fishery for prawns around Shetland. They landed 130 boxes of prawns one week, the catch being marketed by Pioneer Seafoods.

There were more changes in 1992 as a degree of faith returned to the industry after the trauma of previous years. In April the 87ft Campbeltown built *Connaught II* arrived for skipper Robert Irvine and partners of Whalsay. Their previous vessel, the *Prevail*, built in 1986 was exchanged as part of the deal with skipper Stephen Green and partners of Fraserburgh.

In June Jim and Richard Scott of Skeld acquired the very fast *Alert II*, a Cyfish 33 built of GRP by Cygnus Marine. She was powered by a 320hp engine making her the fastest boat in the shellfish sector.

The dangers still inherent in lobster fishing were seen in April when Thomas Christopher Robertson aged 40, of Isbister, Whalsay was drowned when his 19ft lobster boat *Quest* sank as he was shifting creels because of a fresh south-easterly wind.

A departure that summer after a short stay in Shetland was the Banff registered purse seiner *Coronella II*. Built in Norway in 1966 she had been bought by the Altaire Fishing Company for her fishing entitlement which was added to that of the *Altaire*. Stripped of her quota she was sold to a fishing company in Namibia.

The Anderson brothers from Skerries, from left: Greig, David and James, owners of the *Sette Mari*.

In July the 93ft long *Sette Mari* was bought from Sweden by John David Anderson of Skerries and his sons Greig, John David and James. With an engine of 1280hp she was bought for trawling in deeper water. The family still retained the *Alison Kay*.

The Braer

Hopes for a less traumatic year in 1993 were dashed on Tuesday 5th January when the American owned oil tanker *Braer*, carrying a load of crude oil from Norway to the USA, broke down off Sumburgh Head and was driven ashore at Garths Ness where her entire cargo was spilled into the sea.

123

The implications for Shetland's seafood industry were horrendous and it could have tarnished the name "Shetland" for years had it not been for very astute handling of the crisis, for which all three sector of the fisheries industry must take credit.

Three days after the grounding the Shetland Fishermen's Association and the Shetland Salmon Farmers' Association declared an exclusion zone, banning fishing and the harvesting of salmon within coastal waters around the southern half of Shetland. This voluntary ban was followed by a similar announcement by the Government. These moves were aimed at protecting the reputation of Shetland seafood and allaying the fears of consumers.

On this occasion the weather came to the aid of the industry. During the two weeks after the grounding the wind blew a gale from between west and south-west so that all the oil was trapped in the right angle formed by the South Mainland of Shetland and the West Mainland. It was driven northwards as far as Burra, Trondra, Scalloway and Whiteness, causing millions of pounds of damage to the many salmon farms in that area but sparing all the rest of the fishing ground and salmon farms around Shetland.

Shetland Seafood Quality Control and the North Atlantic Fisheries College performed a vital task with their thorough programme of testing both catches and premises and reassuring the public that Shetland fish coming onto the market was of the highest quality. Scalloway fish market was closed for several weeks but the market at Lerwick continued as normal.

When the situation was known to be under control those affected began to consider their losses and the leaders of the three sectors put forward claims totalling many millions of pounds. The SFA alone helped to negotiate the payment of around £15 million to its members, as compensation for lost fishing opportunities and reduced catches.

The first step in the return to normality came on Friday 23rd April, 1993, when the Government announced the lifting of the ban on catching white fish within the exclusion zone, although the ban on catching shellfish there remained in force for much longer.

Skipper Jeemie Robb and son Brian, successful fishermen in the inshore league.

Photo – J. R. Nicolson

After the Braer

The *Braer* oilspill had no long term effect on the local fishing industry and 1993 saw a return to normal. In March 1993 the white fish trawler *Aquila* was sold to owners in Fraserburgh and her owners Ivor and Graham Polson along with James John Shearer found a replacement in the 109ft long Swedish trawler *Santos* – an indication of renewed interest in deep water fishing.

In April the 24ft long shellfish boat *Quantus* was purchased by Tammie Williamson of Whalsay; and Jeemie and Brian Robb of Scalloway acquired the *Mamre*, a Cygnus 44 which they renamed *Meridian*. The Whalsay white fish vessel *Starina* changed hands when she was bought from David Anderson of Whalsay by Brian Pottinger and partners of Lerwick. Another inshore boat the *Harvest Home* was bought by Michael Adamson of Cunningsburgh.

There was a feeling of regret when the 39ft long *Reliance* sank off the south entrance to Yell Sound on 9th June. Built in Macduff, she was fishing for scallops when her gear became snagged in the seabed and the jolt displaced her engine from its mountings. The *Reliance* was taken in tow by the *Planet* but sank before she could reach safety. Her crew – Ronnie Young (skipper) and Stanley Wood – were rescued by the *Planet*.

Another acquisition from Sweden that summer was the big white fish trawler *Still Waters* (ex-*Tirana*) bought by John Anderson and partners of Scalloway. The previous *Still Waters* was renamed *Zenith* after being sold to a new Whalsay partnership headed by Stuart Kay.

A smaller Swedish vessel the *Carmita* was bought by Colin Hughson and partners of Skerries, to replace the *Horizon* which was sold to another Skerries partnership – Ewan Anderson (aged 21) and his father Willie Anderson.

The Skerries vessel *Carmita*.

The three large Swedish vessels came with no track record of fishing to add to the POs entitlement and membership of the PO would have meant a reduced quota for other members. While building up a track record they had to work in the "non-sector", where quotas were allocated by the Government from a share of the national quota reserved for this purpose. The Board of Directors of the Shetland PO subsequently agreed to admit these vessels into membership even though they had no track record fishing performance. The PO, however, also stated that no more boats would be allowed to join the PO unless they had an historic fishing performance.

Unfortunately these boats proved to be barely viable on the grounds around Shetland and after a relatively short time they returned to Sweden.

More boats joined the local fleet in 1993. Michael Henderson and partners from Yell bought the 78ft long white fish trawler *Heatherbelle IV* from Eyemouth. Her former skipper Billy Aitcheson had bought the Burra boat *Wave Sheaf*. Skipper Henderson's previous boat, the *Discovery* helped to maintain the balance at Burra when it was bought by Charles Moffat and partners, the young skipper's first command.

Another change of ownership took place in Skerries when father and son,

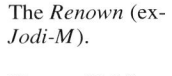

The *Renown* (ex-*Jodi-M*).

Photo – K. Murray

both named John William Anderson, bought the 55ft long *Jodi M* as a replacement for the *Renown*, which was sold to David Johnson of Vidlin.

An addition to the Scalloway fleet from Peterhead was the 40ft *Cornucopia* (ex-*Boy James*) for Ronnie Young to replace the *Reliance*, while another smart looking boat for a Burra crew was the *Helenus* for Jerry Pottinger and Steven Henderson.

Owners of the *Helenus* Jerry Pottinger and Steven Henderson.

There was another incident in August when the *Whispering Hope* fouled her propeller and ran aground at the entrance to Gruting Voe. Owned by Russell Smith, she was on hire to brothers Stanley and Stephen Gray who were rescued by the coastguard helicopter.

In October the Adenia Fishing Company, which had operated the small purse seiners *Adenia* and *Advance*, sought a larger vessel to operate with the combined licences of the smaller vessels, both of which were sold to a fishing company in Namibia. The Whalsay partnership found a replacement in Iceland – the 187ft long *Petur Johnsson* which had been built in Norway in 1987. On her arrival at Lerwick she was renamed *Adenia II*. The year ended with the arrival of the 44ft scallop boat *Dunlin* for Sam Davies of Scalloway.

More changes took place in 1994 when some old vessel's left Shetland and some were scrapped under the Government's decommissioning scheme. Skipper Bert Laurenson of Hamnavoe sold his boat the *Radiant Star* which he had acquired in 1964. Still in good condition, she started a new career as a cabin cruiser in the USA. Her successor, renamed *Radiant Star* was the *Evening Star* belonging to Davie Smith of Scalloway and Andrew Smith of Lerwick, both of whom had decided to leave the fishing industry.

Bert Laurenson.

For Bert it had been a hectic few months, starting in November 1993 when he was awarded the MBE for his services to the fishing industry, including 14 years as chairman of the SFA. He was replaced as chairman by John Garriock in 1991, with Mackie Polson as vice-chairman. Mackie was also the holder of the MBE, as was Duncan Robertson, who as managing director of LHD Ltd had been a loyal member of the association's executive committee for many years and had also served as one of Shetland's two representatives on the executive committee of the Scottish Fishermen's Federation. Richie Simpson of LHD replaced Duncan on the association and federation executive committees. The other association representative to the federation was John Goodlad who was actually elected as one of the two vice presidents of the Scottish Fishermen's Federation in 1993. John Goodlad's election to the post of vice president reflected the changed relationship between the association and the federation. From being in a postion of seriously contemplating resignation from the federation in the early 1980s, the association had now become one of the federation's most powerful and supportive constituent associations.

Duncan Robertson.

Another old boat that left Burra about this time was the *Orion*. Like the *Radiant Star* she had been bought by the local PO so that her track record could remain in Shetland being "ring fenced" as a quota within a quota – one which would remain the property of the PO.

John Garriock.

The *Unison*, *Opportune* and *Dee Dawn* were decommissioned, being broken up at the Malakoff. While the *Unison* was a very old boat, built as an MFV during the war, the *Opportune* had been built in 1967 as the *Evening Star* and could have had many years fishing ahead of her.

There were several additions to the fleet in 1994 starting with the large scallop boat *Lista*, bought by Billy MacDonald of Scalloway, working with his brother John. In March the 87ft long white fish trawler *Harvest Hope* was

The *Rival*, skipper
Andrew Goodlad.

Photo – K. Murray

bought by John Anderson and partners of Whalsay, replacing the smaller
vessel *Contest*, which was bought by Richard Gray of Yell. Completing this
chain reaction the 16 metre *Chelaris* was bought by Garry Buchan of
Lerwick, whose previous vessel *Aquarius* was bought by Andrew Leiper of
Mossbank.

The *Altaire*, the
largest tank ship in
the UK fleet.

Photo – K. Murray

April saw an important addition to the white fish fleet in Burra when the
88ft stern trawler *Rival* was bought by Andrew Goodlad and partners. She
was one of four vessels built at Campbeltown for Faroese owners and was
formerly named *Smari*.

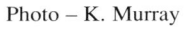

In May the 80ft long beam trawler *Elly Gerda* was bought by Stephen and Stanley Gray from her previous owners in Cornwall for scallop fishing. She was a powerful vessel towing 12 dredges on each side.

The most spectacular vessel to arrive that year was the new *Altaire*, 243ft long and powered by a 6000hp engine. She was equipped for trawling, carrying her catch of herring or mackerel in refrigerated seawater tanks with a capacity of 2500 tonnes, making her the biggest tank ship in the UK. Another change in the pelagic sector was the retirement of skipper Josie Simpson and the sale of the *Azalea* to the Research Fishing Company as a pair trawling partner with the *Research*.

Quick thinking allied to training in life-saving contributed to the survival of the five-man crew of the white fish trawler *Adonis*, when she sank with her gear out 60 miles west-north-west of Foula on Wednesday 22nd June, 1994, after fire had broken out in her engine room. Skipper Trevor Cumming and crew had barely time to get their life-jackets on when the vessel went down. They were rescued by the crew of the *Endeavour* (skipper Jeemie Fullerton) and brought ashore by the Sumburgh based coastguard helicopter. As a result of this rescue in difficult conditions skipper Fullerton and crewmembers Ellis Johnson, David Robertson, David Nicolson, Geoff Hunter and Steven Simmons were presented with certificates by the Royal Humane Society.

The *Adonis* was one of the biggest white fish trawlers in Shetland. Built at Campbeltown in 1985 she was 85ft long but was lengthened on the Scalloway slip with in additional seven feet section at the stern.

Duncan Cumming and his sons Trevor and Angus wasted no time in looking for a replacement which they found in Orkney, when they acquired the 90ft long *Nordfjordr*, built in 1989 by Millers of St Monans.

Another addition to the fleet that year was the 65 ft long *Heritage* bought by David Riley of Burra and Gordon Jamieson of Walls. A number of shellfish boats joined the fleet in the second half of 1994. The *Moontan* was acquired by John Moncrieff of Scalloway and sold soon afterwards to Kenneth MacLennan of Lerwick, while John A. Ratter of Cunningsburgh bought the *Gadus* from owners in Peterhead, Russell Smith of Burra bought *My Rose Ann* and Sam Davies of Scalloway added another vessel to his previous purchase the *Dunlin*. Around this time David Selbie and partners of Lerwick acquired the Teignmouth registered *Seven Sisters*. Towards the end of the year Ronnie Johnson of Eshaness bought the Cygnus hulled *Chantelle* while another Cygnus, the *Stephanie*, arrived at Whalsay for Bobby Sandison.

The growth in the shellfish fleet at this time was due partly to the compensation for lost earnings paid by the oil pollution fund following the *Braer* incident.

The value of fish landed by UK vessels at Shetland ports reached a new record of nearly £29.5 million in 1994 – a rise of £5.8 million compared with 1993. There was a big rise in the catch of scallops – from 473 tonnes in 1993

Arnold Goodlad skipper of the scallop boat *Kelly Ann*.

Photo – C. Lund

to 637 tonnes, while the value rose to over £1 million due to increased effort. There was also a big rise in the catch of brown crabs – up from 221 tonnes to 351 tonnes while the catch of velvet crab increased from eight tonnes in 1993 to 44 tonnes due to an excellent demand for this species in France and Spain.

There was a big rise in herring landings from 31,214 tonnes in 1993 to 44,879 tonnes and the rise in the mackerel catch was even more spectacular – from 58,278 tonnes to 79,205 tonnes valued at £10,438,000, thanks to exceptionally heavy landings in January and February while the shoals were still in the Shetland area.

There were important changes in the pelagic sector in 1995 with the arrival of two "super" trawlers, the *Serene* and *Charisma* for Whalsay crews, replacing older vessels of those names.

First to arrive on Monday 19th June was the *Serene*, built in Norway at the yard of Flekkefjord Slip and Maskinfabrikk A/S to a design by Skipsteknisk A/S of Alesund. She was 57.2m (188ft) long with a beam of 12m and a minimum draught on 6.5m. Her big Wartsila Wachmann engine delivered 2900hp. While the previous *Serene* was equipped for both trawling and purse seining, the new vessel was designed solely for trawling, carrying two Swan nets (made in Ireland), one with a fishing circle of 1000 metres, the other of 1650 metres. Her nine refrigerated tanks had a capacity of around 1000 tonnes. Two weeks later the *Charisma* arrived from the Simek yard at Flekkefjord, only one foot longer than the *Serene* and almost identical to design and equipment.

This was the start of a remarkable period in the history of the fishing industry in Whalsay, with the building of five vessels having a total value of close on £50 million. In October 1996 the new *Antares* was launched from Flekkefjord Slip and Maskinfabrikk. She was 211ft long and had cost around £9 million. A month later an identical vessel the *Zephyr* was completed at the same yard, designed for operating independently or as a pair trawling partner with the *Antares*. The fifth vessel was the *Research*, built by Slippen mek Verksted in the north of Norway at a cost of £9 million.

The crew of the *Research* on arrival in Lerwick after the launch. Back row, from left: Magnus Sandison, Nigel Tulloch, Alec Fullerton, David Nicolson, Harry Sandison, Richard Williamson, Jeemie Sandison, Garry Williamson, Willie Hutchison, Alec Wishart and Willie Williamson. Front row, from left: Alec John Polson, Michael Williamson, Harry Sandison and Arthur Williamson.

130

The 1995 herring season was the best for several years, helped by the reopening of the fishery for Atlanto-Scandian herring, which had been closed for several years in an attempt to aid the recovery of this stock after years of overfishing. It gave Shetland Catch an early start that year with landings by Danish and Icelandic purse seiners.

The Shetland Fishermen's Association had fought for several years to obtain an EU – and therefore UK share in this fishery which had previously been the monopoly of the Scandinavian nations. The SFA had pointed out that this stock had provided the "winter" herring fishery for Shetland vessels between the wars. As a result of this claim the Shetland PO eventually obtained an annual quota of around 12,000 tonnes of Atlanto-Scandian herring.

There were still more changes in the shellfish fleet at this time. In 1995 the *Sarah Lena* was bought from Newhaven by Robbie Leask of Lerwick to be operated by him and his son Gary. In 1996 Stanley and Stephen Gray, having sold one of their beam trawlers, purchased a suction dredger to start a fishery for razor shells. They soon found that the local stock could not support a commercial fishery of this type.

The Norwegian built *Aquarius* changed hands again when Andrew Leiper sold her to Sidney Johnson of Brae to replace her with the *Golden Grain*. The *Tranquility* found a new owner that year, being sold by John Garrick to Calum Irvine of Weisdale, while Sam Davies sold the *Rosa Jade* and replaced her with the *Loch Innes*.

Peter Jamieson, skipper of the Whalsay boat *Korona*.

Photo– Deborah Lamb

Moves of fundamental importance were afoot that year in the white fish sector as three crews, having watched developments in north-east Scotland, with a new generation of twin-rig stern trawlers, designed for fishing in deeper water, along the edge of the continental shelf, placed orders for new vessels.

These moves led to the sale of Robbie Watt's *Andromeda II* to a Whalsay partnership, headed by Bobby Sandison, who renamed her *Arcturus*. Plans by John Garriock and partners to acquire a larger vessel to replace the *Sunbeam* led first to the purchase of the old stern trawler *Vega* from Ian Walterson and partners. Ian and the vessel's engineer Billy Hughson decided to purchase the Lerwick firm HNP Engineers, along with Billy's father Hugh Hughson, an original partner in the business.

As the new vessel neared completion in Spain the *Vega* was taken to Denmark to be scrapped, while the *Sunbeam* was bought by Stuart Kay and partners of Whalsay and renamed *Auriga*. That partnership then sold its previous vessel *Zenith* to a new partnership headed by James Burnett of Lerwick.

An interesting addition to the Burra fleet was the 23m long steel-hulled stern trawler *Lomur*, bought by Gary Smith and partners, while Alex Simpson and partners bought the *Sceptre*, both vessels operating through West Side Fishermen Ltd. Another change took place

The third generation *Sunbeam*, built for John Garriock and partners.

Photo – K. Murray

at Skerries when the *Starina*, formerly owned by skipper Brian Pottinger of Lerwick and partners, was bought by Ewan Anderson and partners, while their previous boat the *Horizon* started a new career on the west coast of Scotland. Another two vessels to leave Shetland in 1996 were the *Discovery* and *Korona*, both of which went to Ireland.

The three "new generation" white fish trawlers were launched in the summer of 1997. First was the *Sunbeam*, launched at the Astilleros Zamacona yard at Bilbao – a massive ship 143 feet long, her main engine developing 2610hp while her hold could carry 2000 boxes of fish, if filled to capacity.

Only a few days later the *Andromeda III*, a 28.3m long vessel for skipper Robbie Watt and partners was launched at Macduff. The third of the new class was the *Vandal* for Duncan Cumming and his sons Trevor and Angus. She was a 33.9m vessel built at the Parnica yard in Poland.

The *Andromeda III* built for skipper Robbie Watt and partners.

There were more changes in the local fleet in 1997. In May Jeemie and Brian Robb acquired the 52ft long stern trawler *Crystal Sea* from previous owners in Eyemouth and renamed her *Fraoch Ban*. In June the *Valhalla* arrived in Skerries to replace the *Starina*, while Leslie Gray of Yell bought his fifth shellfish boat the *Valkyrie*, a Cygnus GM40, to replace the *Sincere V* which then went to Pittenweem. At the very end of that year Michael Henderson and partners from Yell bought the twin-rig trawler *Solstice* to replace the smaller *Heatherbelle* which was bought by a Whalsay crew to replace the much older *Langdale*.

While the general trend of this period was to invest in larger more powerful white fish trawlers, there was also a counter trend towards smaller vessels less expensive to operate, equipped with more selective types of fishing gear to catch better quality fish.

This trend started in September 1996 when James Anderson from Skerries bought the small gill-netter *Joanne Claire*. Early in 1998 Ivor Polson, formerly skipper of the *Santos*, had the 9.97m long *Lindisfarne* built in Norway, equipped for trawling, purse seining and jigging; and she was followed a few weeks later by another two inshore boats built in Norway, the *Utsker* and *Solan* for brothers David and Greig Anderson.

However there is a major difference between Shetland and Norway in that the Norwegian Government has sea areas reserved for small boats using static gear, whereas in the UK trawling is permitted practically up to the beaches.

Another interesting move in 1998 was the decision by Alex Hutchison and partners of Whalsay to have the trawler *Achieve* converted for gill netting, while David Robertson and partners bought the Peterhead registered *Constant Friend* for gill netting, their previous vessel, the white fish trawler *Endeavour*, being sold to a Peterhead partnership.

This trend has been influenced by the increasing scarcity of fish on traditional grounds, high operational costs and the amount of effort required to make a profitable catch, with vessels working round the clock on weekly trips with alternate crews to make this operation possible.

Chapter Ten

Half a century of progress

In September 1997 Shetland Fishermen's Association celebrated its 50th anniversary with a dinner dance in Lerwick Town Hall. Secretary John Goodlad listed a long series of achievements – the negotiations with the oil industry in the 1970s; the prolonged negotiations that preceded agreement on the Common Fisheries Policy; the establishment of an office at Brussels and the subsequent reshaping of the CFP; the setting up of Shetland's own PO in 1982; the association's response to the Braer oilspill; and the part the association played in the setting up of the North Atlantic Fisheries College.

Shetland's fishermen meet at the North Atlantic Fisheries College for an A.G.M. in 1994.

In Mr Goodlad's opinion the association's main achievement during the first half century was to represent the interests of all Shetland fishermen, regardless of the type of fishery or the size of vessel.

In 1996 the association adopted a new internal structure with the executive committee being served by three sub-committees, representing each of the pelagic, white fish and small boat sectors. Mackie Polson of Whalsay was elected the chairman of the pelagic committee, David Anderson of Skerries is the white fish sub-committee chairman while Billy Hughes (m.v. *Tussan*) is chairman of the sub-committee representing the interests of smaller boats. Josie Simpson took over from John Garriock as chairman of the association in 1996. With Mackie Polson being elected chairman of the pelagic sub-committee, there was a vacancy for the post of vice chairman of the association. This position was filled by Bert Laurenson. Josie Simpson and Bert Laurenson had of course both previously served as chairmen of the association and therefore provided the association with a very experienced team.

The association's membership now stands at 120 vessels, the largest number in its history. The composition of the fleet has changed considerably with far fewer (but much larger) pelagic vessels and many more shellfish boats. Such has been the growth in the latter sector, the association has taken the initiative, with other local organisations, to regulate inshore fisheries using the new concept of a Shetland Regulating Order.

The controversy between fishermen and environmentalists was the backdrop to an intense debate in the 1980s over the sandeel fishery. In 1997 the association reached an agreement with the Royal Society for the Protection of Birds and Scottish Natural Heritage on a new management regime for this fishery, which is based on local regulation. This is a very rare example of fishermen and environmentalists agreeing a joint policy for the management of a controversial fishery.

An enormous change has taken place in the inshore white fish sector, where only a small number of vessels are still working the seine net. They include the *Pilot Us* from Scalloway, still owned by the Watt family – the only vessel to have been in membership throughout the association's 50 years. This change has had a drastic effect on the volume of fish landed at Scalloway.

The end of another successful haul for the inshore seine netter *Pilot Us* – one of many thousands during her 50 years in Shetland.

While certain issues have caused disagreement within the association these have usually been resolved quite easily. The biggest split emanated from the Common Fisheries Policy, which has led to deep divisions in the fishing industry throughout the UK.

From this dispute emerged the Save Britain's Fish (SBF) campaign, which sought to take Britain out of the CFP with each state resuming responsibility for the management of its own sea area. It highlighted the CFP's failure to conserve stocks, its adverse impact on small fishing communities and the mass of regulations which can be exploited by unscrupulous fishermen. It also predicted that there would be an influx of Spanish and Portuguese vessels into the North Sea where they have no historic rights to fish.

Critics of the SBF campaign pointed to the success of the CFP – notably stability in market prices and European funding for fishing vessels, processing plants and harbours. They argued that the principle of relative stability gives the UK very substantial quotas with the lion's share of mackerel, haddock, monkfish and prawns. It was also pointed out that no political party would ever support unilateral withdrawal from the CFP.

On 21st May, 1994, the leaders of Save Britain's Fish, Tom Hay, chairman of the Scottish White Fish Producers' Association and John Ashworth, well known for his numerous letters in the fishing newspapers, presented the case for CFP withdrawal in a debate in Lerwick's Garrison Theatre. The opposing view was put by Willie Hay, past president of the Scottish Fishermen's Federation and John Goodlad. The debate was chaired by association chairman, John Garriock.

At a special meeting of the SFA's executive committee, held in the North Atlantic Fisheries College on 31st January, 1995, it was agreed that a referendum should be held to determine the association's response to the Save Britain's Fish campaign. It was agreed that members should vote on two issues – withdrawal from the CFP or reform of the CFP while remaining in membership.

After a postal ballot the result was declared in 1st April, 1995. Only 152 fishermen (39 per cent) were in favour of withdrawal, while 241 fishermen (61 per cent) voted for reform.

With this clear mandate John Goodlad was appointed chairman of a special committee set up by fisheries minister Michael Jack to put forward proposals for a review of the CFP.

The infrastructure

As the Shetland fishing fleet expanded, shore facilities, the responsibility of many different firms and bodies, have developed to meet its needs. In 1947, when the association was formed, the facilities at Lerwick consisted of the small boat harbour south of Victoria Pier and the privately owned docks in the North Harbour. Alexandra Wharf provided space for the herring fleet during the summer. Now the huge Morrison Dock caters for all sectors of the fleet, from shellfish boats to large super trawlers.

Alexandra Wharf is still used extensively by white fish vessels to haul out their nets for repair; and during bad weather the whole area north of Victoria Pier is usually crowded with British and foreign fishing vessels.

The fish market on Laurenson Quay proved to be too small for the catches of the 1980s and it was extended, being reopened by Scottish Fisheries Minister Sir Hector Monro on 12th March, 1993. Originally 55m long it was extended by 28 metres. It is now in three sections, each of which can be chilled independently.

Much of the facilities provided initially for the oil industry is now used by the fishing industry, the Shetland Catch processing plant being a perfect example, while its quays are used for berthing pelagic trawlers between fishing seasons. These vessels also use the former oil industry base at Dales Voe to haul ashore their huge trawls for repair and maintenance.

Lerwick Harbour Trust's pilot boats *Ord* and *Bard* proved inadequate for the tasks demanded of them. The *Ord* was replaced in 1980 by the *Knab*, a vessel purpose-built in Norway and designed for towage, fire fighting and salvage work. In 1990 the pilot boat *Kebister* was built by James N. Miller & Sons of St Monans to replace the *Bard*.

The amalgamation of Malakoff Ltd at Lerwick and William Moore & Sons at Scalloway in the early years of the oil boom provided a better service for the fishing and oil industries. While the Malakoff Slipway, now under cover, still provides a service for small and medium sized vessels, a large floating dock, which arrived in 1989, caters for the larger vessels. At Scalloway the old Prince Olav Slipway still handles small boats while a larger slip caters for bigger vessels.

Vast improvements were made at Scalloway in the 1980s after the Blacksness Pier Trust had handed over its assets and obligations to Shetland Islands Council. In 1980 a large breakwater was built to the east of the old harbour, extending into the East Voe.

Plans for reclamation to the north of the breakwater were delayed as objections were raised – mainly by conservation groups outwith Shetland – over the potential impact on the setting of Scalloway Castle. A public inquiry resulted in victory for the council and work on the second phase of the project began in 1982.

It included a refrigerated fish market, with space on the first floor for a net loft, chandlery store and offices for West Side Fishermen Ltd and a smaller chandlery store and an office for LHD Ltd. The project cost £4.1 million, of which 40 per cent was provided by the council while the Department of Agriculture and Fisheries and the EU each provided 30 per cent of the funding.

Developments at Whalsay did not keep pace with the growth of the fleet, causing anger among local fishermen, led by their able councillor Henry Stewart. When the breakwater and quay built in 1964 was found to be

Henry Stewart (seated) with the Whalsay fishermen during a campaign for better pier facilities at Symbister.

Photo – D. Coutts

inadequate an inner jetty was built for the use of small boats. Eventually a rubble breakwater was built to the west of the original one, allowing vessels to berth on both sides of the old one.

The introduction of purse seining led to demands for an improvement, as the island soon had eight of these vessels, accounting for one fifth of the entire Scottish pelagic fleet. Once again the harbour was far too small and councillor Stewart began his long battle to achieve adequate facilities.

The first phase began in 1989 when Haka (UK) deepened the inner and outer basins and constructed a rubble breakwater on the east side of the harbour, all at a cost of £1.54 million. Work on the second phase began in 1991, the contract awarded to the Belgian firm Herbosch Kiere. It consisted of a solid sheet-piled face along the inner side of the new rubble breakwater, 140m long and 20m wide, built at a cost of £2.3 million.

Among the smaller harbours West Burrafirth was able to jump the queue because of unforeseen events. In 1981 the council was forced to act to save the ferry service to Papa Stour, following the tragic loss of the small boat which had provided a link with Sandness.

Captain Gordon Walterson, the councillor for the area, had a long discussion with local people and it was agreed that West Burrafirth, with its better shelter, should become the Mainland terminal for this service.

Most of the Whalsay pelagic fleet in harbour taking advantage of the new facilities.

Photo – K. Murray

Clark Diving Services started work in August 1984 and the new harbour was ready in July the following year, after expenditure of nearly £500,000. It was clearly a pier in the right place, as small seine netters working in St Magnus Bay began to land their catches there, while the smaller shellfish boats which had been operating from West Burrafirth for several years, found the new facilities a vast improvement. In 1988, according the Scottish Sea Fisheries tables, 211 tonnes of white fish, valued at £140,000 and 186 tonnes of shellfish valued at £128,000 were landed there.

A revival of the fishing industry at Northmavine brought with it the need for improvements at Collafirth. Shetland Islands Council became involved in 1985 when it bought a partially built pier and caused consternation when it decided to demolish the pier for safety reasons.

Clark Diving Services started work in September 1987 and the pier was opened on 14th December, 1989, by Chris Dowle, the councillor for the area. The local fishing vessels *Altaire* and *Aspire* had stopped fishing to be present. This is the *Altaire*'s berth between fishing seasons and her presence here causes surprise among visitors who round a corner in a rather infertile part of the islands to find one of the UK's largest fishing vessels lying comfortably at a modern harbour.

Cullivoe was next on the council's list for harbour improvements. One of the old herring jetties had survived until 1972 when it was replaced by a new pier of similar construction, shortly after the introduction of the roll-on roll-

The *Altaire* and the *Endeavour* use the new pier facilities at Collafirth.

off ferries. These enabled local and visiting boats to land their catches at Cullivoe for transport to markets at Lerwick or Scalloway.

The main drawback at Cullivoe was lack of shelter and this was partly rectified by the building of a rubble breakwater a short distance farther south.

The campaign for a safe harbour received a boost in July 1984 when Peterhead Harbour Trustees called for improvements at Cullivoe to make it

The UK's most northerly fishing harbour at Cullivoe, Yell.

Photo – Ian Leask

safer for boats from the north-east of Scotland, fishing to the north of Shetland, to shelter there.

Plans for a much larger and stronger pier were drawn up by the council's Department of Design and Technical Services, which was hard pressed to cope with all the projects planned at this period. It was decided to build the new pier as an extension to the breakwater. It was formally opened on 5th July, 1991, by councillor David Johnston, a champion of the fishing industry throughout Shetland. Since then improvements have been carried out to the harbours at Burravoe in Yell, Skerries and Baltasound, providing vastly improved facilities for the fishermen based in those areas.

The association could take considerable satisfaction from the fact that the quality of harbours and piers developed throughout Shetland reflected very closely the association's piers policy during the 1980s and 1990s.

Ancillary firms

The fishing industry could not function without the help of a number of firms providing services in a variety of fields. Essential to the operation are the fish salesmen of whom LHD Ltd is by far the largest. West Side Fishermen has 15 vessels in its books and A. S. Fraser at Scalloway handles the accounts of three small vessels.

Ice is supplied by J. & M. Shearer (Ice Supplies) Ltd, a subsidiary of LHD. The firm has invested heavily in new equipment, supplying tube ice from plants at both Lerwick and Scalloway.

Fishing boats take on ice from J. & M. Shearer's ice plant beside the fishmarket at Scalloway.

Photo – Robert Johnson

The firm undertook a massive development at Shearers Quay after the area had been bought by Lerwick Harbour Trust in 1985. While dredging was being carried out by the harbour trust, to deepen the north entrance to the harbour, all the material recovered was taken ashore and stored until it could be used as infill for a 95 metre long quay. On this site a new ice plant now produces 48 tonnes of tube ice each day.

A smaller plant at Cullivoe provided by Robert Henderson, trading as North Ice, provides a valuable service to fishing vessels in that part of Shetland.

The vast amount of electrical and electronic equipment now in use requires a high level of expertise both in installation and service. H. Williamson and Sons (Scalloway) Ltd is widely recognised as one of the best in the UK. It is now part of the LHD group, as is Oceansafe, the largest net mending firm in the islands.

Apart from the major engineering firms like Malakoff & Moore, HNP Engineers and L. & M. Engineering, there are several smaller firms, some started by one man, offering specialised services.

Magnus Mann started in business as a one-man operation repairing trawl doors. Before long the business expanded as MMW Welding, adding to its original role the supply of ancillary equipment to large pelagic trawlers. The firm also manufactures its own MMW vacuum pumps, which discharge catches of herring and mackerel from the vessel's tanks to the shore.

Jim Johnson of Muckle Roe developed a seine net warp measuring device to ensure that both "sides" of rope were of equal length while fishing. He then went on to develop a similar device for trawlers.

Next he considered how the process of sorting, gutting and washing the catch could be speeded up from the pounds or hopper on the fore-deck to the hold. He designs and manufactures fish handling equipment, made to measure for each boat that orders it. Several of the latest vessels have his equipment on board.

Rescue services

A vital role is played by the Coastguard Maritime Rescue sub-centre at Lerwick. With a staff of 18 it keeps a 24 hour radio watch on VHF and medium wave frequencies and DSC (digital selective calling) – the new computerised distress alert system. Additional help in emergencies comes from 16 auxiliary coastguard companies throughout the islands.

The sub-centre liaises closes with the two RNLI lifeboats at Lerwick and Aith and with the coastguard rescue helicopter based at Sumburgh Airport, which covers an area within a 150 mile radius of Sumburgh.

When survivors are brought ashore they may be taken to the Gilbert Bain Hospital at Lerwick or, more usually, be met by a member of staff of the Lerwick centre of the Royal National Mission to Deep Sea Fishermen, which provides clothing, hot meals and accommodation and arranges transport on the first stage of their journey home.

Occupying a commanding position overlooking Lerwick Harbour, the Mission provides a vital service to fishermen throughout the year, with its restaurant, rest room and recreation room, in addition to cabins for those who require them.

Hundreds of lives have been saved in recent years by the rescue services but sadly there are still fatalities at sea. In January 1998 the creel boat *Accord* from Baltasound was reported overdue, north of Unst. A full scale search was mounted but it failed to find any sign of the boat or her crew – brothers Norman and Cecil Gray.

The Scottish Fisheries Protection Agency

Over the years the staff of the Lerwick Fishery Office have kept a watch on the industry to ensure that Government rules regarding mesh sizes and minimum landing sizes of fish are observed. They had a difficult job when industrial fishing was at its peak, as they examined catches to check whether by-catch limits were being exceeded.

During the period of klondyking extra staff were drafted in to maintain three shifts, working round the clock, logging fish catches and granting klondyking licences on behalf of the Secretary of State.

Now the fishery officers' job is even more difficult as they enforce the regulations introduced by the European Community, in addition to those introduced by the UK Government.

The fishery officers also give advice on available quotas and fishing areas; rules on technical conservation and fishing gear; fishing licences and their transfers; the registration of vessels; marketing regulations; claims for damage to fishing gear and financial assistance schemes.

Shetland's seafood industry

The fish catching sector is only one third of a vast seafood industry that has developed in Shetland during the last 50 years. The processing sector has developed and diversified to keep pace with the changes in the fishing industry and the production of farmed salmon has increased dramatically from its modest beginnings in 1983. Salmon farming owes a lot to the fishing industry, its development carried out by men who had had years of experience in handling boats, nets and anchors.

Only a few of the original white fish processing plants are still maintaining their original role. At Lerwick L. Williamson still produces laminated block and IQF (individually quick frozen) products for markets in the USA and the UK; and Ronas Fisheries and Whalsay Fish Processors still have their white fish filleting lines.

While Shetland Catch is the main outlet for herring and mackerel, the Shetland Smokehouse at Skeld and McNab's at Lerwick smoke herring, mackerel and white fish, mainly for local markets.

SFA officials and representatives after the 1998 A.G.M. From left: Brian Isbister (Assistant Secretary), John Goodlad (Secretary), Mackie Polson (Pelagic Sub-Committee Chairman), Bert Laurenson (Vice-Chairman), Josie Simpson (Chairman), David Anderson (Whitefish Sub-Committee Chairman) and Marvin Smith (Administration Officer). Missing from the picture is Billy Hughes (Small Boat Sub-Committee Chairman. In the background is the Shetland Seafood Centre where the Association is now based.

Photo – J. Coutts

At Scalloway Danny Watt concentrates on shellfish in the TTF premises vacated by G. & J. Hunter, who now fillets and smokes fish for local markets. The Hunters also buy fish on the local market for shipment to clients on the mainland.

The shipping buyers are a major part of the marketing system in Shetland. One of the biggest was the business built up by Scott Ward after his retirement from fishing. He had been a prominent fisherman and a member of the association's executive committee for several years.

Salmon processing has compensated to a great extent for a downturn in white fish processing. The largest packing station that of Saga Seafoods, occupies the site of the former Iceatlantic processing plant at Scalloway and another large packing station provides a large number of jobs in the West Mainland. The former white fish processing plants at Burra, Skerries and Mid Yell are now involved with packing salmon and Whalsay Fisheries now depends on salmon for much of its production. Just north of the Shetland Catch processing plant at Lerwick another very large salmon packing station is operated by Lerwick Fish Trader.

Shetland Seafood Quality Control, based at the North Atlantic Fisheries College, plays a vital role within the industry under section leader Arthur Nicolson. Regular inspections are carried out at fish markets, on fishing boats and in the processing plants themselves.

Shetland Fishermen's Association, Shetland Fish Processors' Association and Shetland Salmon Farmers' Association are housed in the Shetland Seafood Centre in the prestigious Stewart Building on Lerwick's waterfront, named after the late Henry Stewart, councillor for Whalsay and Skerries. It was opened by his widow Jeannie Stewart on 24th February, 1996. Here too is the office of Shetland Fishing News, the monthly journal which is published by the three sectors of the seafood industry in Shetland.

Billy Hughes (Small Boat Sub-Committee Chairman) on board his shellfish vessel, *Tussan.*

Because of the importance of the seafood sector to the economy of the islands, Shetland Islands Council maintains a close link through Jim Henry, who is their divisional manager – fisheries, formerly skipper of the purse seiner *Wavecrest.*

The North Atlantic Fisheries College is playing an increasingly important role through its training in all three sectors, its work in fisheries research and its recent success in product development. While it has its own inshore fishing trawler Atlantia for training and research, it has also undertaken a new role in developing hatcheries for species which are now overfished in the wild – notably lobsters and halibut. The college is set to become the fisheries and marine science department of the brand new Highlands and Islands University.

In 1996 the value of fish caught by Shetland vessels was estimated at £46 million and 21,000 tonnes of salmon produced by local farmers was worth £54 million and the processing sector added a further £60 million, giving a total of £160 million and emphasising the importance of fisheries to the Shetland economy.

Fifty years of change

Since Shetland Fishermen's Association was formed in 1947 enormous changes have taken place throughout the fishing industry. In 1947 the seine net winch, belt-driven from the fore end of the engine, was the only mechanical device on deck; now a range of hydraulic winches and power blocks handle the heavy gear.

The seine net itself has been largely displaced by the trawl. Many vessels now fish far more effectively with a twin rig, whereby two trawls are towed side by side on three wires wound on three drums. Meanwhile, the purse seine, which so dramatically replaced the drift net in the 1960s, has itself been replaced by pelagic trawling. At the same time, increased mechanisation now allows a small shellfish boat to work twice as many creels as much larger boats did some 35 years ago.

While fishing vessels now spend longer periods at sea, usually with double crews, working alternate weeks, there is greater comfort for the crew. In place of a confined fo'c'sle or cabin, which was used for cooking, eating, sleeping and recreation, modern vessels have well equipped galleys and messrooms with TV sets, CD players etc, while in the latest vessels crewmembers have single or double-berth cabins. It is significant that on the newest vessels crewmen entering the accommodation area from the working deck must remove oilskins and boots.

Fifty years ago remnants of the old superstitions were still alive and older crewmen were horrified if reference was made to land creatures such as rabbits, rats and mice. Those days have gone for ever as is proved by some of the emblems that decorate the sides of wheelhouses – like the depiction of cartoon character Roland Rat on the wheelhouse of a previous *Andromeda*.

Science and technology have replaced the earlier inherited skills in fish finding. The wheelhouse is crammed with the latest equipment to locate fish shoals and identify grounds that can be fished such as echosounders, sonars, track plotters, satellite navigation systems and radar sets.

With increased technology has come the need for more sophisticated training. Shetland is fortunate in having the North Atlantic Fisheries College at Scalloway which provides training of the highest standards. The development of the Fisheries College has paralleled a change in the perception of fishing as a career. For many years, fishing was regarded as an occupation of last resort. This attitude was often particularly marked within the fishing communities themselves. It is perhaps not surprising since fishing was not only a hard occupation but often paid very poorly. This has changed and many young Shetlanders now rightly see the fishing industry as an exciting and challenging career choice.

Despite the escalating costs of fishing boats and licences, the traditional Shetland shareholding system has survived virtually unchanged during the last 50 years. Fishing vessels in Shetland continue to be owned by the majority of fishermen who work on board the vessels. In most fishing communities throughout Europe, the ownership of fishing vessels has become concentrated in the hands of skippers or shore based companies. This has not yet happened in Shetland.

The staff of the Shetland Fishermen's Association thanking the retiring office manager Christine Johnson for all her years of service to the SFA. Back row (left to right): Una Flaws (office manager); Marvin Smith (administration officer); Christine Johnson (office secretary); Karene Williamson (administration assistant). Front row: Brian Isbister (assistant Association secretary); Christine Johnson (retiring office manager); John Goodlad (Association secretary).

Photo – J. Coutts

One interesting change has been the geographical location of fishing vessel partnerships. Fifty years ago boats were owned by partnerships from separate fishing communities such as Burra, Whalsay and Skerries. Now, fishing boats are increasingly owned and crewed by 'Shetland wide' partnerships.

There are new worries however – how to catch enough fish to pay for expensive vessels, leaving a reasonable payment for the crew. The traditional half catch system is still operated by some boats whereby, after certain expenses have been deducted, half the earnings go to the owners of the boat and the other half is divided equally among the crew, some of whom will be partners in the vessel. In the case of larger more expensive vessels a greater proportion goes to 'boat and gear'.

There are tensions unknown to previous generations. Under the Common Fisheries Policy there are rules which are difficult to adhere to. Quotas are set for each species and it is galling to have to dump good quality over-quota fish back into the sea. The alternative is to break the rules and sell the fish privately – the now well known black fish trade.

Fishermen buying a boat also have to purchase a licence from someone who is willing to sell. The trade in licences is one of the most controversial aspects of the fisheries policy. Usually when a boat is sold outwith Shetland the licence and track record go with it. Recently the Shetland PO and Shetland Islands Council have combined forces to build up a community fund of fish quota, which is 'ring-fenced' for the benefit of the local industry.

The past 50 years of the association itself has seen dramatic changes. In 1947 the Shetland Fishermen's Association met infrequently and employed a part-time secretary from his home in Hamnavoe. During the past 50 years the importance of the association and its involvement in all aspects of the fishing industry has undergone a sea change. The association (together with the Shetland PO) now employees a staff of six from its offices in Lerwick. The regular Executive Committee meetings are now complemented by frequent meeting of sub-committees representing the whitefish, pelagic and small boat sectors. This reflects the fact that the association has always tried to cater for all sizes and types of fishing vessel. The Shetland Fishermen's Association,

50 years after it was founded, still represents everything from the smallest to the largest boat in Shetland. This is probably the greatest testimony to its success as the voice of the fishermen of Shetland.

Looking ahead it is difficult to predict the shape of the fishing industry in years to come. Only one thing is certain – Shetland will continue to need its fishing industry with an association to look after its interests. The oilfields around Shetland will run dry eventually but the fish stocks are renewable and can continue to provide the basis for a sustainable fishing industry for future generations of Shetlanders. These Shetland fishermen of the future will find that they will probably have even more need for an association than their predecessors did in the past.

Shetland fishermen – the next generation.

Photo – Deborah Lamb

Chairmen of the
Shetland Fishermen's Association
1947 - 1997

1947 - 1951	John Thomson	m.v. *Blossom*
		m.v. *Silver Cloud*
		m.v. *Norseman's Bride*
1951 - 1953	John W. Leask	m.v. *Wave Sheaf*
1953 - 1955	Jeemie Pottinger	
1955 - 1957	James A. Watt	m.v. *Pilot Us*
1957 - 1958	Robert Watt	m.v. *Harvest Gold*
1958 - 1959	Geordie Hunter	m.v. *Ocean Reaper*
1959 - 1963	John J. Fullerton	m.v. *Brighter Hope*
1963 - 1964	Geordie Hunter	m.v. *Ocean Reaper*
1964 - 1966	Ronnie Aitkin	m.v. *Concord*
1966 - 1969	David Anderson	m.v. *Amethyst*
1969 - 1971	Josie Simpson	m.v. *Good Tidings*
1971 - 1972	Bobbie Peterson	m.v. *Concord*
1972 - 1973	Jeemsie Ward	m.v. *Unison*
1973 - 1975	Jeemie Wiseman	m.v. *Nil Desperandum*
1975 - 1979	Josie Simpson	m.v. *Azalea*
1979 - 1991	Bert Laurenson	m.v. *Radiant Star*
1991 - 1996	John Garriock	m.v. *Sunbeam*
1996 -	Josie Simpson	m.v. *Silver Spirit*

Secretaries of the
Shetland Fishermen's Association
1947 - 1997

1947 - 1975	Jeemie Pottinger
1975 - 1980	Geordie Hunter
1980 - 1981	Arthur Makins
1981 -	John Goodlad

INDEX

INDEX OF FISHERMEN

INDEX OF BOAT NAMES